CONFESSIONS
OF A
MEDICAL
HERETIC

CONFESSIONS OF A MEDICAL HERETIC

ROBERT S. MENDELSOHN, M.D.

McGraw·Hill

New York   Chicago   San Francisco   Lisbon   London   Madrid   Mexico City
Milan   New Delhi   San Juan   Seoul   Singapore   Sydney   Toronto

The *McGraw·Hill* Companies

Library of Congress Cataloging-in-Publication Data

Mendelsohn, Robert S.
    Confessions of a medical heretic.
    Bibliography: p.
    Includes index.
    ISBN 0-8092-4131-5
    1. Iatrogenic diseases.   2. Medicine—Philosophy.   I. Title.
RC90.M46   610   78-73670

18 19 20 21 22 23 24 25 26   DSH/DSH   0

ISBN 978-0-07-183790-3

This book is printed on acid-free paper.

Contents

Acknowledgments

I am grateful:

To my students, now renowned physicians, who have fulfilled the traditional concept of teaching me more than either my colleagues or my professors. Those who have most profoundly influenced me are Mayer Eisenstein, M.D., and Fred Ettner, M.D.

To the late Leroy Fatherree, M.D., public health physician, who 30 years ago introduced me to a critical look at American medicine and through whom I met Herbert Ratner, M.D., who continues to extend this valuable education.

To Marian Tompson, President, La Leche League International, who 15 years ago selected me as a member of her Medical Advisory Board. Her exemplary leadership enabled me to later appreciate David and Lee Stewart, and Gail and Tom Brewer, whose influence saturates this book.

To John L. McKnight, Professor, Urban Affairs Center, Northwestern University, who articulated for me the political and professional truths that provide the setting for my thoughts on medicine.

To Dominick Bosco, who gave wholeheartedly of his spirit as well as his outstanding professional writing skill to this book.

To all who gave me career opportunities which led to my present thinking, and to all who denied me opportunities which I mistakenly thought I wanted.

Above all, to my wife, who surrounded me with the stability, security, protection, and love that afforded me the luxury of thinking and writing.

Non Credo

I do not believe in Modern Medicine. I am a medical heretic. My aim in this book is to persuade you to become a heretic, too.

I haven't always been a medical heretic. I once believed in Modern Medicine.

In medical school, I failed to look deeply into a study that was going on around me, of the effects of the hormone DES—because I believed. Who could have suspected that twenty years later we would discover that DES causes vaginal cancer and genital abnormalities in children born to women receiving the drug during pregnancy?

I confess that I failed to be suspicious of oxygen therapy for premature infants, even though the best equipped and most advanced premature nurseries had an incidence of partial or total blindness of around ninety percent of all low birth weight infants. A few miles away, in a large, less "advanced" hospital, the incidence of this condition—retrolental fibroplasia—was less than ten percent. I asked my professors in medical school to explain the difference. And

I believed them when they said the doctors in the poorer hospital just didn't know how to make the correct diagnosis.

A year or two later it was proved that the cause of retrolental fibroplasia was the high concentrations of oxygen administered to the premies. The affluent medical centers had higher rates of blinding simply because they could afford the very best nursery equipment: the most expensive and modern plastic incubators which guaranteed that all the oxygen pumped in reached the infant. At the poorer nurseries, however, old-fashioned incubators were used. They looked like bathtubs with very loose metal lids. They were so leaky that it made very little difference how much oxygen was pumped in: not enough reached the infant to blind it.

I still believed when I took part in a scientific paper on the use of the antibiotic Terramycin in treating respiratory conditions in premature babies. We claimed there were no side effects. Of course there weren't. We didn't wait long enough to find out that not only didn't Terramycin—or any other antibiotic—do much good for these infections, but that it—and other tetracycline antibiotics— left thousands of children with yellow-green teeth and tetracycline deposits in their bones.

And I confess that I believed in the irradiation of tonsils, lymph nodes, and the thymus gland. I believed my professors when they said that of course radiation was dangerous, but that the doses we were using were absolutely harmless.

Years later—around the time we found out that the "absolutely harmless" radiation sown a decade or two before was now reaping a harvest of thyroid tumors—I couldn't help wondering when some of my former patients came back with nodules on their thyroids: Why are you coming back to me? To *me*, who did this to you in the first place?

But I no longer believe in Modern Medicine.

I believe that despite all the super technology and elite bedside manner that's supposed to make you feel about as well cared for as an astronaut on the way to the moon, the greatest danger to your health is the doctor who practices Modern Medicine.

I believe that Modern Medicine's treatments for disease are seldom effective, and that they're often more dangerous than the diseases they're designed to treat.

I believe the dangers are compounded by the widespread use of dangerous procedures for non-diseases.

I believe that more than ninety percent of Modern Medicine could disappear from the face of the earth—doctors, hospitals, drugs, and equipment—and the effect on our health would be immediate and beneficial.

I believe that Modern Medicine has gone too far, by using in everyday situations extreme treatments designed for critical conditions.

Every minute of every day Modern Medicine goes too far, because Modern Medicine *prides itself* on going too far. A recent article, "Cleveland's Marvelous Medical Factory," boasted of the Cleveland Clinic's "accomplishments last year: 2,980 open-heart operations, 1.3 million laboratory tests, 73,320 electrocardiograms, 7,770 full-body x-ray scans, 210,378 other radiologic studies, 24,368 surgical procedures."

Not one of these procedures has been proved to have the least little bit to do with maintaining or restoring health. And the article, which was published in the Cleveland Clinic's own magazine, fails to boast or even mention that any people were helped by any of this expensive extravagance. That's because the product of this factory is not health at all.

So when you go to the doctor, you're seen not as a person who needs help with his or her health, but as a potential market for the medical factory's products.

If you're pregnant, you go to the doctor and he treats you as if you're sick. Childbirth is a nine-month disease which must be treated, so you're sold on intravenous fluid bags, fetal monitors, a host of drugs, the totally unnecessary episiotomy, and—the top of the line product—the Caesarean delivery!

If you make the mistake of going to the doctor with a cold or the flu, he's liable to give you antibiotics, which are not only powerless against colds and flu but which leave you more likely to come down with worse problems.

If your child is a little too peppy for his teacher to handle, your doctor may go too far and turn him into a drug dependent.

If your new baby goes off his or her feed for a day and doesn't gain weight as fast as the doctor's manual says, he might barrage your breastfeeding with drugs to halt the natural process and make room in the baby's tummy for man-made formula, which is dangerous.

If you're foolish enough to make that yearly visit for a routine examination, the receptionist's petulance, the other patients' cigarette smoke, or the doctor's very presence could raise your blood pressure enough so that you won't go home empty-handed. Another life "saved" by antihypertensive drugs. Another sex life down the drain, since more impotence is caused by drug therapy than by psychological problems.

If you're unfortunate enough to be near a hospital when your last days on earth approach, your doctor will make sure your $500-a-day deathbed has all the latest electronic gear with a staff of strangers to hear your last words. But since those strangers are paid to keep your family away from you, you won't have anything to say. Your last sounds will be the electronic whistle on the cardiogram. Your relatives *will* participate: they'll pay the bill.

No wonder children are afraid of doctors. They *know*! Their instincts for real danger are uncorrupted. Fear seldom actually disappears. Adults are afraid, too. But they can't admit it, even to themselves. What happens is we become afraid of something else. We learn to fear not the doctor but what brings us to the doctor in the first place: our body and its natural processes.

When you fear something, you avoid it. You ignore it. You shy away from it. You pretend it doesn't exist. You let someone else worry about it. This is how the doctor takes over. We let him. We say: I don't want to have anything to do with *this, my body and its problems*, doc. You take care of it, doc. Do what you have to do.

So the doctor does.

When doctors are criticized for not telling their patients about the side effects of the drugs they prescribe, they defend themselves on the grounds that the doctor-patient relationship would suffer from such honesty. That defense implies that the doctor-patient relationship is based on something other than knowledge. *It's based on faith.*

We don't say we *know* our doctors are good, we say we have *faith* in them. We *trust* them.

Don't think doctors aren't aware of the difference. And don't believe for a minute that they don't play it for all it's worth. Because what's at stake is the whole ball game, the whole ninety percent or more of Modern Medicine that we don't need, that, as a matter of fact, is out to kill us.

Modern Medicine can't survive without our faith, because Modern Medicine is neither an art nor a science. It's a religion.

One definition of religion identifies it as any organized effort to deal with puzzling or mysterious things we see going on in and around us. The Church of Modern Medicine deals with the most puzzling phenomena: birth, death, and all the tricks our bodies play on us—and we on them—in between. In *The Golden Bough*, religion is defined as the attempt to gain the favor of "powers superior to man, which are believed to direct and control the course of nature and of human life."

If people don't spend billions of dollars on the Church of Modern Medicine in order to gain favor with the powers that direct and control human life, what do they spend it on?

Common to all religions is the claim that reality is not limited to or dependent upon what can be seen, heard, felt, tasted, or smelled. You can easily test modern medical religion on this characteristic by simply asking your doctor *why?* enough times. Why are you prescribing this drug? Why is this operation going to do me any good? Why do I have to do that? Why do you have to do that to me?

Just ask *why?* enough times and sooner or later you'll reach the Chasm of Faith. Your doctor will retreat into the fact that you have no way of knowing or understanding all the wonders he has at his command. *Just trust me.*

You've just had your first lesson in medical heresy. Lesson Number Two is that if a doctor ever wants to do something to you that you're afraid of and you ask *why?* enough times until he says Just Trust Me, what you're to do is turn around and put as much distance between you and him as you can, as fast as your condition will allow.

Unfortunately, very few people do that. They submit. They allow their fear of the witch doctor's mask, the unknown spirit behind it, and the mystery of what is happening and of what will happen, to change into respectful awe of the whole show.

But you don't have to let the witch doctor have his way. You can liberate yourself from Modern Medicine—and it doesn't mean you'll have to take chances with your health. In fact, you'll be taking less of a chance with your health, because there's no more dangerous activity than walking into a doctor's office, clinic, or hospital *unprepared*. And by *prepared* I don't mean having your insurance forms filled out. I mean you have to get in and out alive *and* accomplish your mission. For that, you need appropriate tools, skills, and cunning.

The first tool you must have is knowledge of the enemy. Once you understand Modern Medicine as a religion, you can fight it and defend yourself much more effectively than when you think you're fighting an art or a science. Of course, the Church of Modern Medicine never calls itself a church. You'll never see a medical building dedicated to the religion of medicine, always the medical *arts* or medical *science*.

Modern Medicine relies on faith to survive. All religions do. So heavily does the Church of Modern Medicine rely on faith that if everyone somehow simply forgot to believe in it for just one day, the whole system would collapse. For how else could any institution get people to do the things Modern Medicine gets people to do, without inducing a profound suspension of doubt? Would people allow themselves to be artificially put to sleep and then cut to pieces in a process they couldn't have the slightest notion about—if they didn't have faith? Would people swallow the thousands of tons of pills every year—again without the slightest knowledge of what these chemicals are going to do—if they didn't have faith?

If Modern Medicine had to validate its procedures objectively, this book wouldn't be necessary. That's why I'm going to demonstrate how Modern Medicine is not a church you want to have faith in.

Some doctors are worried about scaring their patients. While you're reading this book, you are, in a sense, my patient. I think you *should* be scared. You're supposed to be scared when your well-being and freedom are threatened. And you are, right now, being threatened.

If you're ready to learn some of the shocking things your doctor knows but won't tell you; if you're ready to find out if your doctor is dangerous; if you're ready to learn how to protect yourself from your doctor; you should keep reading, because that's what this book is about.

1
Dangerous Diagnosis

I don't advise anyone who has no symptoms to go to the doctor for a physical examination. For people *with* symptoms, it's not such a good idea, either. The entire diagnostic procedure—from the moment you enter the office to the moment you leave clutching a prescription or a referral appointment—is a seldom useful ritual.

The mere act of delivering yourself to the priestly doctor and submitting to his wishes presumably bestows the benefit. The feeling is that the more exams you have, and the more thorough the exams, the better off you'll be.

All of which is nonsense. You should approach the diagnostic procedure with suspicion rather than confidence. You should be aware of the dangers, and that even the simplest, seemingly innocuous elements can be a threat to your health or well-being.

The diagnostic tools themselves are dangerous. The *stethoscope*, for example, is nothing but the priestly doctor's religious badge. As a tool, it does more harm than good. There's no question that there's a high degree of contagion from the use of stethoscopes from patient to patient. And there's almost no form of serious disease that cannot be suspected or diagnosed *without* the stethoscope. In congenital heart disease where the baby is blue, it's obvious because the baby is blue. In other forms of heart disease, the diagnosis can be made by feeling the various pulses around the body. In coarctation of the aorta, for example, there's a deficiency of the pulse rate in the femoral arteries in the groin. You don't need a stethoscope to make that diagnosis.

The only value of the stethoscope over the naked ear applied to the chest is in the convenience and modesty of the physician. There's nothing that he can hear with the stethoscope that the physician cannot hear with his ear against the person's chest. As a matter of fact, I know some doctors who now put the stethoscope around their neck and don't put the ear pieces in their ears as they apply the bell to the patient's chest! At one time I used to think that was really terrible. Not any more. The doctor probably realizes, consciously or otherwise, that the patient needs the stethoscopic examination because it's part of the sacred ritual rather than because it makes any sense or does any good.

And it can do harm, expecially in the case of children. Suppose a mother brings her daughter in for her annual exam. The child has no symptoms of illness whatsoever. But the doctor uses the stethoscope and discovers a functional heart murmur—a harmless heart sound found in at least one third of all children at one time or another. At that point the doctor has to make a decision whether or not to tell the mother. Now at one time doctors used to keep this information to themselves. They might put it in the chart in symbolic form so that nobody but a doctor could read it. Recently, doctors have been taught to share this information with the parents, either because of their belief in the patient's right to know or—more likely—because they're afraid another doctor will find it and tell them first.

So the doctor tells the mother. And whether or not he reassures the family that the murmur is innocent, both mother and daughter may suspect—perhaps for the rest of their lives—that something really *is* wrong! Mother may then begin a trek to pediatric car-

diologists who will take repeated EKGs, chest x-rays, or even perform cardiac catheterizations to help the mother "get to the bottom
of all this." Studies have shown that families of children with heart
murmurs tend to do two things: They restrict their child's activity
and do not allow them to play in sports, and they encourage them to
eat more. Naturally, these are the worst things they can do! They
literally make cardiac cripples out of their children.

Though it's a lot more impressive than the stethoscope, the electrocardiogram (EKG) is little more than an expensive electronic toy
for the physician. More than twenty years ago a survey revealed that
the reports of expert EKG interpreters varied by twenty percent
among individuals and by another twenty percent when the same
individuals re-read the same tracing at another time. Time of day,
recent activity, and many other factors besides the condition of one's
heart can affect the readings. In one test the EKG delivered a positive finding in only twenty-five percent of cases of *proven* myocardial
infarction, an equivocal finding in half, and a totally negative
finding in the rest. And in another test, more than half of the readings taken of healthy people were grossly abnormal.

Yet physicians and other medical personnel continue to increase
rather than decrease their reliance on the EKG as a detector of cardiac problems. I have a recurring fantasy of a person lying in an intensive coronary care unit after suffering a heart attack. He is perfectly comfortable—until he's approached by a nurse with a
hypodermic syringe. She explains that his EKG monitor has shown
an irregularity that demands immediate treatment. Of course, she is
not aware of the studies that show the high degree of error in electronic monitoring equipment, or the studies that show the not-
infrequent leakage of electricity from one monitor to another in the
same ward. My fantasy patient protests and pleads with the nurse:
"Please, nurse, feel my pulse. It's absolutely regular!" The nurse's
answer is that there's no point in feeling his pulse. You can't argue
with the machine. So she immediately plunges the needle in his
arm. You can guess at the outcome.

My fantasy is not so fantastic as you might think. There are electronic monitors in "advanced" coronary units that are equipped to

electrically "correct" the heartbeat of patients who, the machine decides, need a jolt. I have heard of cases where the machine decided the person needed a jolt when, in fact, he didn't.

While the electroencephalogram (EEG) is an excellent instrument for the diagnosis of certain kinds of convulsive disorders and the diagnosis and localization of brain tumors, not many people are aware of its limitations. About twenty percent of people with clinically established convulsive disorders never have an abnormal EEG. Yet fifteen to twenty percent of perfectly normal people have abnormal EEGs! To demonstrate the questionable reliability of the EEG as a measure of brain activity, one researcher connected one in the standard manner to a mannequin's head filled with lime jello and got a reading indicating "life."

Despite these obvious possibilities for error, the EEG is used as the primary diagnostic tool in determining whether or not a child truly has organic learning difficulties, minimal brain damage, hyperactivity, or any of the twenty or thirty other names assigned to this ill-defined syndrome. Despite the fact that every pediatric neurologist in need of publishing a paper has reported some significance of this spike or that dip, there has been a total lack of agreement on a valid correlation between an EEG reading and a child's behavior.

Nevertheless, this lack of scientific validation has in no way interfered with the proliferation of EEG machines and the skyrocketing numbers of EEGs performed. I often recommend to students in search of a career the entire field of electroencephalography since it, like everything else connected with learning disabilities, is a growth industry. Today educators, physicians, and parents have consciously or otherwise joined in a conspiracy to medicalize almost all behavior problems. What happens is that a child gets sent home with a note asking for a conference. At the conference, the parents are told the child might have an organic brain problem, might be hyperactive, might be minimally brain damaged. Parents and child are hustled off to the doctor for an EEG. Then, on the basis of the EEG—which may or may not be accurate—the child is drugged into fitting the behavior mold that best suits the teacher.

By far, the most pervasive and dangerous diagnostic tool in the doctor's office is the x-ray machine. Unfortunately, because of its great religious significance, the x-ray machine will be the hardest for doctors to give up. They know that people are awed by the doctor's power to see right through their flesh, to gaze firsthand at what is afflicting them, to see where they cannot. Doctors literally got drunk on this power and started using x-rays on everything from acne to settling the mysteries of the developing fetus. Many obstetricians still insist on x-rays if they don't quite trust their skill in determining fetal position by palpation—despite the fact that childhood leukemia has a well-documented link with prenatal radiation exposure.

Thyroid lesions, many of them cancerous, are now turning up by the thousands in people who were exposed to head, neck, and upper chest radiation twenty to thirty years ago. Thyroid cancer can develop after an amount of radiation that is less than that produced by ten bite-wing dental x-rays. Scientists testifying before Congress have emphasized the hazards of low level radiation to both the present generation and to future generations in the form of genetic damage. They have implicated x-rays in the development of diabetes, cardiovascular disease, stroke, high blood pressure, and cataracts—all associated with aging. Other studies have matched radiation to cancer, blood disorders, and tumors of the central nervous system. Conservative estimates peg the number of deaths each year directly attributable to medical and dental radiation at 4,000.

As far as I'm concerned, these deaths are unnecessary, as is the host of other afflictions attributed to radiation. A quarter century ago, I was taught in medical school that x-rays of the breast were practically worthless. A recent survey showed that things haven't changed very much. Physicians supposedly trained to interpret mammograms were no more accurate than untrained physicians in spotting breast cancer on mammograms. A survey more than thirty years ago showed that as many as twenty-four percent of radiologists differed with each other interpreting the same chest film, even in cases of extensive disease. Thirty-one percent of them even disagreed with themselves when re-reading the same films! Another study in 1955 showed that thirty-two percent of chest x-rays showing definite abnormalities in the lungs were misdiagnosed as negative. In 1959, thirty percent of the experts disagreed with other experts on radiographic readings, and twenty percent disagreed with themselves when re-reading the same films! A 1970 Harvard study showed that the going rate of disagreement among radiologists was still at least twenty percent.

Yet x-rays are still sacred in most doctors' and dentists' offices. Hundreds of thousands of women are still lining up every year for breast x-rays, despite the well published scientific evidence that the mammography itself will cause more breast cancer than it will detect! The ritual of the annual x-ray, the pre-employment x-ray, the school entrance x-ray, and the health fair x-ray continue. I hear about and get letters from people whose doctors pronounce them in perfect health, but still insist on a chest x-ray. One man told me about going to the hospital for a hernia operation, where he was given *six* chest x-rays. From the radiologists' conversations, he got the distinct impression they were experimenting with the exposure levels. This same man was given thirty x-rays at a local dental school where he went to get a crown replaced.

Many doctors defend their use of x-rays on the grounds that the patients demand or expect x-rays. To that excuse, I reply that if people are addicted to x-rays, the greatest service doctors might perform would be to rig up machines that look and sound like real x-ray machines. A tremendous amount of disease could be avoided.

Lab tests are another part of the diagnostic procedure that do more harm than good. Medical testing laboratories are scandalously inaccurate. In 1975, the Center for Disease Control (CDC) reported that its surveys of labs across the country demonstrated that ten to forty percent of their work in bacteriologic testing was unsatisfactory, thirty to fifty percent failed various simple clinical chemistry tests, twelve to eighteen percent flubbed blood grouping and typing, and twenty to thirty percent botched hemoglobin and serum electrolyte tests. Overall, erroneous results were obtained in more than a quarter of all the tests. In another nationwide survey, fifty percent of the "high standard" labs licensed for Medicare work failed to pass. A large scale retesting of 25,000 analyses made by

225 New Jersey labs revealed that only twenty percent of them produced acceptable results more than ninety percent of the time. Only half passed the test seventy-five percent of the time.

To get some idea of what people are really getting for their $12 billion worth of lab tests each year, thirty-one percent of a group of labs tested by the CDC could not identify sickle cell anemia. Another test group incorrectly identified infectious mononucleosis at least one third of the time. From ten to twenty percent of the tested groups incorrectly identified specimens as indicating leukemia. And from five to twelve percent could be counted on to find something wrong with specimens which were healthy! My favorite study is one in which 197 out of 200 people were "cured" of their abnormalities simply by repeating their lab tests!

If you think these tests are shocking, keep in mind that the Center for Disease Control monitors and regulates fewer than ten percent of the country's labs. So these tests indicate the best work of the best labs. With the rest, you pay your money and you take your chances. And you *will* pay more and more, because doctors practicing "just in case medicine" are ordering more and more laboratory tests.

As long as these tests have such an immense possibility for inaccuracy, the only way to look at them is as sacred oracles or fortune telling rituals: they depend on the whims of the deities and the skill of the magician-priest. Even if the deities are keeping up their end of the bargain and your tests results are miraculously correct, there is still the danger that the doctor will misinterpret them. One woman wrote me that at her last routine examination, a test revealed blood in her stool. Her doctor subjected her to every possible test, including barium x-rays, all of which proved negative. The doctor did not give up. Though the woman was in real pain because of the tests, he recommended further testing. Six months later, his diagnosis was announced to a much weakened woman: she had too much acid in her stomach!

Lab tests and diagnostic machines wouldn't be so dangerous if doctors weren't addicted to the quantitative information these tools provide. Since numbers and statistics are Modern Medicine's language of prayer, quantitative information is considered sacred, the word of God, indeed, the *last* word in a diagnosis. Whether the tools are simple, like thermometers, scales, or calibrated infant bottles, or complicated, like x-ray machines, EKGs, EEGs, and lab tests, people and doctors are dazzled into crowding out of the process their own common sense and the qualitative judgment of doctors who are real diagnostic artists.

Scales cause all kinds of trouble in pediatrics and obstetrics. The pediatrician weighs the baby and gets all upset if the baby doesn't gain a certain amount of weight. Again, he's substituting a quantitative evaluation for a qualitative one. The important questions are: What does the baby look like? What's his behavior? How does he look at you? What are his movements like? How's his nervous system functioning? Rather than relying on these observations, the doctor goes by the numbers. Sometimes a breastfed baby won't gain as fast as the doctor mistakenly thinks it should. So he puts the baby on formula—to the detriment of both mother and baby.

Pregnant women also should pay no attention to the scale. There is no correct amount of weight for any mother to gain. Again, the important evaluations are qualitative rather than quantitative. She should be eating the right food, not merely "correct quantities" of any food. If she's careful about what she eats, how much she eats will take care of itself. She'll rightly be able to ignore the scale.

Calibrated infant formula bottles are another menace. The pediatrician tells the mother to make sure the baby gets "*x*" amount at every feeding, and, by golly, she's determined to stick to that goal. So at every feeding she cajoles, threatens, and in some way gets that exact amount out of the bottle and into the baby. Most of the time the baby will throw most of it back up, anyway. The net result is a lot of bad feelings between mother and baby—a lot of anxiety and tension where there should be love and enjoyment. Not to mention a good chance of obesity in later life.

Temperature taking is virtually useless, too. The first question a doctor asks a mother over the telephone when she calls to complain about an illness is what is the child's temperature. This question has no meaning because there are innocuous diseases that carry very high fevers. Roseola, for example, is a common disease of infancy, absolutely harmless; yet it frequently carries a temperature of 104 or 105. On the other hand, there are life-threatening diseases, such as tuberculous meningitis and others, that carry no fever at all or even a subnormal temperature. The doctor should be asking for qualitative information, such as how the child is feeling and what the mother has noticed in his behavior. The reliance on numbers is simply to validate the whole process for religious purposes. Because it is merely a useless ritual, mothers should answer the physician's question about temperature by saying, "I don't know; I haven't taken it." Or, "I don't have a thermometer in the house." Of course, the doctor then thinks they're kooks or health nuts or mentally deficient, so I tell mothers instead just to pick out a fictitious number. If you really want to command the doctor's attention, pick out a high number, 104 or anything within the realm of credibility. Then if the doctor comes over and finds the temperature is normal, right on the button, 98.6, you can say, "Oh it was so much higher before!" If the doctor doesn't believe you, the only thing he can accuse you of is misreading the thermometer. You can even volunteer that remark by saying, "I might have misread the thermometer!" Then, once you get by the sacred quantitative barrier of the thermometer, you and the doctor can move on to more important things.

One of the common dangers of going in for an exam is that you'll be used for purposes other than your own. Years ago, after becoming director of an outpatient clinic I found out that one of the routine questions asked of mothers was "Is your child toilet trained?" Every boy who was not toilet trained by the age of four was separated out and referred for a urological workup, which included, among other things, a cytoscopy. All these four-year-old kids were being cytoscoped! I immediately eliminated the question about toilet training. It didn't take long before I got a call from the chairman of the urology department, who happened to be a friend of mine. He was very angry. First he told me I had done the wrong thing eliminating the question and, thereby, the urological workup. He said it was important to do this kind of examination in order to find the rare cases in which there might be something organically wrong. Well, of course that was nonsense, because all the rare cases can be identified by measures that are far less dangerous than a cytoscopy.

Then he told me more about what was going on. The real problem was that I was destroying his residency program because in order for a residency to be approved by the accrediting authorities, the residents have to perform a certain number of cytoscopies every year. In this case it was around 150. I was taking away his source of cytoscopies, and I got into trouble over it.

This is true for other specialties, too. In order to have a cardiology residency approved, the resident must perform a minimum number—150, 200, 500, whatever it is—of catheterizations every year. There is a great tendency to take people off the street and identify them as needing a cardiac catheterization!

Because of the increased danger of being used for the doctor's own purposes, it's best to regard any doctor who does research or teaching as potentially harmful. As far as I'm concerned, a doctor treating a person should be a treating doctor. Leave the research and teaching to someone who is identified as a researcher or a teacher. When a doctor mixes roles he has to be extremely careful. And so does his patient.

Naturally, the most sinister and dangerous ulterior purpose you expose yourself to is the doctor's need to recruit patients. Without the ritual of the checkup, internists would have trouble paying the office rent! How else can the doctor ensure a steady supply of sacrificial victims for the Church's other sacraments without the examination? The Gospel said many were called and few were chosen, but the Church of Modern Medicine has gone that one better: *All* are called and *most* are chosen.

Annual physicals were once recommended for such high-risk groups as industrial workers and prostitutes. However, today many doctors recommend that *everybody* have at least one a year. In the last fifty years of regular checkups, however, not a shred of evidence has emerged to show that those who faithfully submit live any longer or are any healthier than those who avoid doctors. Because of the definite risks involved, I'd say those that stay away are better off.

In no uncertain terms, you're at the doctor's mercy. The fact that you're there in the first place means you don't know *how* you are or what is going on with *you* and that you want the doctor to tell you. So you're ready to give up a precious liberty, that of self identification. If he says you're sick, you're sick. If he says you're well, you're well. The doctor sets the limits of what's normal and abnormal, what's good and what's bad.

If you could rely on the doctor's conception of normal and abnormal, sick and well, submitting to him would be scary enough. But you *can't* rely on it. Most doctors are unable to recognize wellness, simply because they're not trained in wellness but in *disease*. Because they have sharper eyes for signs of disease than for signs of health, and because they have no conception of the relative importance of signs of both in the same person, they're more apt to pronounce you sick than well.

As long as the doctor is in control, he can define or manipulate the limits of health and disease any way he chooses, narrowly or broadly—depending on *his* intentions and interests. In this way, he can manipulate the amount of disease. For example, he can define high blood pressure as anything above *or* within the high range of normal. And he can treat it accordingly—often with very powerful drugs. Disease can thus be defined to encompass small or large numbers of the population. If he measures 100 children's height, he can state that any child standing at either extreme—in the lowest and highest one, two, or five percent—is "abnormal" and *requires further testing*. He can set his outer limits of normal blood or urine values or electrocardiogram readings, so that a certain percentage of each population is labeled *possibly abnormal, requires further investigation*.

If he were selling laxatives, he would tend to define constipation in such a way as to include the great majority of Americans, by saying that if a person doesn't have a good bowel movement once a day, he or she is constipated. On the other hand, if he's interested in the truth, he would say that if a person has normally formed bowel movements, it doesn't make a difference if they have them once or twice a week. That puts almost nobody in the "sick" category.

The doctor can define sickness even where no sickness exists. After all, among those 100 children measured for height, among those blood, urine, and electrocardiogram measurements, *someone* has to be at the extreme high and low ends of the scales. And there are very few people in whom a battery of thirty or forty tests will not reveal at least one "statistical abnormality" which can then lead to an entire series of potentially damaging and disabling medical events.

You have to consider—and beware of—the doctor's self interest. Doctors almost always get more reward and recognition for *intervening* than for not intervening. They're trained to intervene and do something rather than observe, wait, and take the chance the patient will get better all by himself or go to another doctor. As a matter of fact, one of my key pieces of subversive advice to medical students is this: To pass an exam, get through medical school, and retain your sanity, always choose the most interventionist answer on a multiple choice test and you're more likely to be right. For example, suppose somebody says to you that the patient has a pimple on his nose, and asks what should you do? If the first answer is watchful expectancy, wait and see what happens for a few days, that's wrong, reject that. But if one of the answers is cut off his head and hook him up to a heart lung machine, then resew all the arteries and give him twenty different antibiotics and steroids, that answer is right. This piece of advice has carried more of my students through various crucial examinations, including national boards and speciality exams, than any other lesson.

As a patient, once you submit to a physical examination, your doctor might interpret minor abnormalities—real or bogus—as *pre*-conditions of some serious illness, requiring, of course, serious *pre*-intervention. A minor fluctuation on a blood sugar test might be interpreted as *pre*-diabetes, and you'll get some medicine to take home. Or the doctor may find something—maybe a stray tracing on the EKG caused by a passing jet plane—that leads him to believe you have a *pre*-coronary condition. Then you'll go home with a *pre*-

coronary drug or two, which while fighting your *pre*-condition will mess up your life through striking alterations in behavior and mental status, including blurred vision, confusion, agitation, delirium, hallucinations, numbness, seizures, and psychosis.

Maybe you'll get a prescription for *Atromid S,* a "cholesterol-lowering" drug, which, besides possibly lowering your cholesterol, could also give you one or more of these side effects: fatigue, weakness, headache, dizziness, muscle ache, loss of hair, drowsiness, blurred vision, tremors, perspiration, impotence, decreased sex drive, anemia, peptic ulcer, rheumatoid arthritis, and lupus erythematosis. Of course your doctor is not likely to read you this list from the prescribing information that comes with the drug. And he's even less likely to tell you the contents of the paragraph that's set in a black border: "It has not been established whether drug-induced lowering of cholesterol is detrimental, beneficial, or has no effect on the morbidity or mortality due to atherosclerotic coronary heart disease. Several years will be required before scientific investigations will yield the answer to this question."

What kind of person will take that drug after reading that information?

What must be the most common pre-treatment for *pre*-disease is what happens when you go in and the doctor finds your blood pressure a little high. Ignoring the fact that your hypertension might be temporarily caused by your very presence in the office, you'll most likely leave with some sort of anti-hypertensive drug. Though you'll receive little in the way of relief from it, you might get something else: side effects ranging from headaches, drowsiness, lethargy, and nausea, to impotence. In 1970, the Coronary Drug Project Research Group found that these drugs produced an excess number of adverse effects such as non-fatal infarction and pulmonary embolism—and that these effects were *not* outweighed by any trend towards reduced mortality.

Doctors started hawking the importance of the physical examination during the Depression of the 1930s—for all the obvious reasons. For the same obvious reasons, dentists are beginning to hustle people into their offices for routine checkups. I got an announcement the other day from an establishment dental organization that every child should be examined on his third birthday by a dentist and on his seventh birthday by an orthodontist. These exams certainly will not do very many children any good, and they will definitely do most of them harm. Not only from the mercury pollution characteristic of dental offices, the sacramental x-rays, and the Holy Water flouride applications—but from the treatments themselves. The sharp dental explorer that dentists use to examine teeth has been shown to actually inoculate various bacteria from infected teeth to healthy teeth. Orthodontia is still a mysterious and unproven art. We know that a lot of people get into gum problems later in life because of orthodontia early in life. We also know that a lot of people who are recommended for orthodontia and don't get it find that their teeth straighten out all by themselves. Although the recommended exams most probably won't do you or your child any good, they certainly will be good for the dentist or orthodontist.

From my experience, doctors—and dentists, especially—get very defensive about the regular checkup. I've known dentists to refuse to see patients in emergencies because the person hadn't been in for a regular checkup within the past six months! Of course, this attitude gives doctors and dentists the right to play the big game in medicine, *Blame The Victim*. Rather than admit that their sacraments are useless, the magic nonexistent, they can always tell you that you came to them too late.

You can never go to the doctor too soon, most doctors would claim. And most people seem to believe that. You must realize, however, that the mere act of submitting to the diagnostic procedure implies that you're asking for treatment, at least as far as the doctor is concerned. In no uncertain terms, if you show up, you're asking for it. You're asking to be exposed to the whole range of sacramental treatments, from aspirin to ritual mutilation. Of course, the doctor is going to tend towards the more intense forms of sacrifice, since these increase his sacred stature. Some lean so heavily in that direction that they miss completely the lower extreme of possibilities. A young friend of mine took up the challenge of a 100-mile bicycle race, something he'd never done before. About a third of the way into the race, he'd already made up his mind that he wasn't trained for this sort of punishment—but some passing cyclists jeered at him for his slow pace. That made him angry, and he vowed to finish the race, which he did. The next day he woke up and could hardly move. His knees had taken the brunt of the punishment. He was in such discomfort that he went to a doctor. After examining him and taking x-rays, the doctor let him know that he had either gonorrhea or some kind of cancer of the knee. My friend, who had told the doctor about the 100-mile ride, asked whether that didn't have something to do with his condition. The doctor said, *"Not at all,"* and wanted to refer him to a specialist. Of course, my friend didn't even bother to take the referral home with him. In a matter of days, his legs were as good as new.

Some doctors blame the patients for *demanding* treatment for conditions that will take care of themselves. They use the excuse that people show up wanting antibiotics to knock out colds, or powerful and dangerous anti-arthritics for mild joint stiffness, or hormone pills for teenagers to fight acne or stifle growth. I don't accept this excuse. Patients demand a lot of things such as more considerate care, more natural healing techniques, and discussion of alternatives—and doctors rarely give in on *these* issues.

If you want to defend yourself, you've got to understand that the doctor's standards are different from yours and that his are no better. Doctors aren't considerate of the fact that their very questions imply the need for treatment. I counsel doctors not to tell patients about harmless heart murmurs, large tonsils, umbilical hernias—almost all of which will disappear by the sixth birthday. I tell doctors not to ask mothers of three-year-old boys whether or not the child is toilet trained because that automatically makes the mother think there's something wrong with her child if he's not toilet trained.

There are lots of other attitudes and strategies you need to learn if you want to defend yourself against the dangers of the diagnostic procedure. Of course, if it's an emergency such as an accident, injury, or acute appendicitis, you have no choice. But these situations account for only five percent of medical situations. If you have no symptoms at all, you've got no business going to the doctor in the first place. If you do have symptoms, if you *are* sick, then your first defense is to become more informed about your problem than the doctor. You've got to learn about your disease, and that's not very hard. You can get the same books the doctor studied from, and chances are he's forgotten most of it. You can find books written for laymen on just about every disease you're likely to have. The idea is to find out as much about it as possible so you can discuss your problem on an equal—or better—informational footing with the doctor.

Whenever a lab test is prescribed, look up the test and find out what it's supposed to show. Ask the doctor what the test is supposed to demonstrate. Your doctor won't tell you this, but if you do your own detective work, you'll find out that the simple tests such as the blood counts, urine analyses, tuberculin tests, and chest x-rays are so controversial and difficult to interpret that their usefulness is extremely limited.

You should also try to find a lab which maintains a high degree of accuracy. If a lab won't talk about its rate of errors, scratch it off your list. If a lab boasts perfect or near perfect accuracy, be suspicious. But keep asking questions. How do they know they're so accurate? Is the accuracy certified? By whom? You might never find a lab that satisfactorily answers all your questions. If you do, insist that your doctor use that lab. You might have tough going here, because a lot of doctors have a financial interest in certain testing laboratories. Insist. If your doctor does all his own testing, ask the same questions that you would ask a lab. Finally, if a serious course of treatment hinges on the results of lab tests, have them done again at another lab. Even if you have to have them done again at the *same* lab, have them repeated.

The most important way to subvert the diagnostic procedure for your own protection is to ask the doctor questions. In some cases, he'll answer the questions. That's the rare exception. In most cases, the doctor will get upset. Ask the questions anyway—short of getting yourself thrown out of his office. From his attitude and his responses, you can judge him as a human being and get an idea of his expertise.

Questioning can come in handy to protect yourself from x-rays.

Of course, the best protection is no radiation at all. Breast x-rays for women under fifty, women with no symptoms, and women with no history of breast cancer in their family are unjustifiable for the detection of breast cancer. And they're of dubious value to all other women, since the breasts are especially sensitive to x-rays. Any woman can avoid x-rays merely by telling the doctor she thinks she might be pregnant—whether she is or not. Sometimes, as happened to the wife of one of my colleagues, claiming you're pregnant will provoke them into requiring a pregnancy test, too! My friend's wife avoided *that* by telling the nurse-inquisitor that she wanted her husband to perform the test, since this was her first baby and they wanted to keep as much of the event to themselves as possible. She never had to get the x-ray. You can get away with a similar ploy by merely saying you want your own doctor to perform the pregnancy test. Then, rely on bureaucratic inertia to keep the question from ever coming up again. A woman who *is* pregnant, or who truthfully thinks she may be, should make her condition clear by speaking up loudly to anyone who tries to aim an x-ray machine in her direction. Any doctor or dentist who insists on needlessly radiating a pregnant woman should have his license pulled.

Techniques for avoiding x-rays can range from playing dumb— Do I really need all those x-rays, doc?—to persuasion and cajolery. Sometimes these will work, but you should be prepared to resort to direct challenge and confrontation. Sometimes a doctor will have you placed on a cart to be wheeled into the x-ray room. This is a typical ploy to deliberately humiliate, depersonalize, and demean perfectly capable men and women and transform them into docile, cooperative, accepting, manageable patients. If this ever happens to you, jump off the cart and stand on your own two feet. Exercise responsibility for your own health. Any disability you suffer from jumping off the cart will doubtlessly prove less than the effects of the x-rays.

Once you've made known your preference for avoiding x-rays, if your doctor still wants you under the gun, here are the questions you should ask: What are you looking for? What is the likelihood that you will find it using the x-rays? Can you find what you are looking for by a safer method? Are you using the most modern and well-maintained machines with the lowest possible dose of radiation? Will you properly shield the rest of my body? In what way will the x-rays change my course of treatment? When was the last time your machine was checked for safety? Keep asking questions until the doctor explains the situation in such a way that allows you to make an informed choice. If you decide that you must have the x-rays, submit to only the specific photos necessary at the time. Don't let either your doctor or the radiologist shoot extra photos "as long as you're on the table."

To fully protect yourself from your doctor, you must learn how to lie to him. This is not such a strange maneuver, really, since anyone who has learned to survive professional bureaucracies has learned to deceive professionals. You learn to lie to school teachers quite early in life, since the purpose of going to school isn't to learn but to end up with a credential at the end. Then you do all your real learning outside of school. I advise medical students to learn the arts of hypocrisy and duplicity, just as Southern blacks once learned the art of shuffling. Shuffling was the fine art of appearing to be active and obedient when in reality you were nothing of the sort. That's what you have to do with your doctor.

If you are a mother who wants to breastfeed, for example, your doctor will almost always be against it, even if he says he doesn't care one way or the other, because doctors know nothing about breastfeeding. What do you do when your doctor weighs the baby and finds it hasn't gained as much weight as his chart says it should? What do you do when he tells you to start hot dogs at two weeks of age? My favorite image is that of the obstetrician waiting, and as the baby emerges from the womb he sticks a hot dog in its mouth to get it started on solid foods and to create an early dependence. Well, when a doctor tells you to start solid food such as cereal or fruit or anything else at one month of age, you can *try* arguing with him since you know what's best for your baby better than he does. You can simply refuse to do it, in which case he'll get huffy and probably fire you as a patient. You can try to persuade or cajole the doctor, on the assumption that he's a rational, caring human being. If you try that, good luck.

Or, you can shuffle. Don't tell the doctor anything but Yessir. If he has given you a six-pack of formula to take home and start the baby on, throw it in the trash at your earliest convenience. Simply continue to breastfeed your baby. When the next checkup comes around and the doctor puts the baby on the scale, just tell the doctor how the child's enjoying his cereal and fruit. Then the doctor will look at the scale and tell you the baby's doing just fine.

Unfortunately, in some medical situations you reach the point where you can't lie to the doctor. In obstetrics, the doctor gets a chance to see what you're doing. He can check on you with the scale and enforce his dangerous ideas on limiting the amount of weight you gain during pregnancy. Many women will bring a list of what they want and don't want to the obstetrician on the first visit. They'll tell him they don't want to be shaved, no episiotomy, analgesia, induction of labor, and so on. The doctor will nod his head. Then, in the final moments of labor, she'll find out that she's getting them anyway. You can't really expect a woman in labor to say no to whatever her doctor says she needs.

That's why it's crucial to subvert the process and get the jump on the doctor as much as possible before the situation gets critical. After you've asked your questions, don't take it for granted that you can trust the doctor's answers. Check out whatever he says. Again, read all the sources you can find. You have to know more about it than he does.

Doctors in general should be treated with about the same degree of trust as used car salesmen. Whatever your doctor says or recommends, you have to first consider how it will benefit *him*. For example, if a neonatologist tells you that high risk nurseries improve the survival rates of babies, find out if he works for a high risk nursery.

Whenever you get a second opinion that is different from the first opinion, you should go back and confront the first doctor with what the second doctor said. People don't often do this because they're afraid of the anger and hostility of the first doctor. It's very valuable to test the doctor this way. It's a good idea to elicit that anger and hostility because that might change your attitude towards the doctor. And towards doctors in general.

Whenever you have to make a decision regarding a medical procedure, you should seek out and talk to people you regard as having wisdom. At one time, if you go back far enough, doctors were wise, cultured people. They knew literature and culture and were marked by sagacity and consideration. That is not the case any more. People who may be a source of information and counsel are people who have had the same experience as you, people with the same symptoms or disease. Talk over your problem, whatever your doctor tells you it is and whatever *you* think it is, with friends, neighbors, and family. Find out what their doctors say. Doctors tell you not to do this, not to listen to opinions you hear in the butcher shop or the grocery store or the hairdresser's. They tell you not to listen to relatives and friends. But they're wrong. They're protecting their sacred authority. As a matter of fact, you *should* talk to friends and relatives, people who live around you, whom you know and trust, at the *outset* of your symptoms.

You may find you can do without the doctor.

2
Miraculous Mayhem

I can still remember how, early in my medical career, I gave intravenous penicillin every few hours to children who were suffering the agonizing symptoms of bacterial meningitis, and then watched miraculous changes occur hour by hour. Children who had been on the verge of death recovered consciousness and began to respond to stimuli within a few hours. A few days later those same children were back on their feet, almost ready to go home.

Patients with lobar pneumonia also would endure terrible agonies. They would enter a crisis of high fever, severe cough, gasping for breath, shaking, chills, and extreme chest pains. Some recovered, but many died. When penicillin came along, people with lobar pneumonia no longer went through a crisis period. Instead, the fever, cough, and other symptoms resolved within days. People who would never have left the hospital alive packed their bags and walked out.

I—and other doctors—truly felt that we were witnessing and *working* miracles.

Things are different today. Meningitis and lobar pneumonia are uncommon. Even when a doctor does come up against such a life-threatening condition, the treatment is so routine that it is mainly carried out by a nurse or a medical technician. While the fascination with the miracle remains, these drugs that were once extremely valuable are now extremely dangerous.

Many doctors prescribe penicillin for conditions as harmless as the common cold. Since penicillin works almost exclusively against bacterial infections, it's useless against viral conditions such as colds and flu. Penicillin and other antibiotics do not shorten the course of the disease, do not prevent complications, and do not reduce the number of pathogenic organisms in the nose and throat. They do no good at all.

What they *can* do is cause reactions ranging from skin rash, vomiting, and diarrhea to fever and anaphylactic shock. If you're lucky, you'll only be one of the seven to eight percent of people who suffer a rash—although a much higher percentage of people suffering from mononucleosis have gotten a rash when given ampicillin. For the unlucky five percent who get serious reactions to penicillin, the picture of a patient in anaphylactic shock is not pretty: cardiovascular collapse with clammy skin, sweating, unconsciousness, fallen blood pressure, disturbance in heart rate and rhythm. It eerily evokes images of the very diseases which penicillin was designed to *cure!*

By no means is penicillin the only villain. Chloromycetin is a drug which is effective in a certain type of meningitis caused by the *H. influenza bacillus,* as well as in diseases caused by typhoid and similar germs. In such situations, chloromycetin is often the *only* antibiotic that will work. But chloromycetin also has the not uncommon fatal side effect of interfering with the bone marrow's production of blood.

When a person's life is at stake anyway, this is an acceptable risk to take. But if a child suffers nothing more than a viral sore throat, is the non-relief chloromycetin will bring worth risking depression of the child's bone marrow, which will require multiple transfusions and other therapies, none of which will guarantee complete recovery? Of course it's not; yet doctors *do* prescribe chloromycetin for sore throats.

Tetracycline became so popular in outpatient clinics and office practices that it became known as the "housecall" antibiotic. It has been widely prescribed for children as well as other age groups because it is effective against a wide variety of organisms and because its side effects are not considered dangerous. But there is a fair list of adverse reactions which the informed person might not choose over the drug's non-use in situations it wasn't designed for anyway. A more formidable side effect is that the drug is deposited in the bones and teeth. While no one knows exactly what tetracycline does to the bones, hundreds of thousands—perhaps millions—of parents and children know that it permanently stains the teeth yellow or yellow-green. Though *you* might feel that's too high a price to pay for the dubious effectiveness of the drug in relieving the symptoms of a common cold, many doctors do not. The current rationalization for the drug's use in such situations is the suspicion that a child who appears to be suffering from a cold might actually have a *mycoplasma* infection. The vast majority of children with a common cold have no trace of this sort of infection.

The U.S. Food and Drug Administration finally woke up to the widespread overuse of tetracyclines in 1970, when it required a warning on all packages of the drug: "The use of drugs of the tetracycline class during tooth development (last half of pregnancy, infancy, and childhood to the age of eight years) may cause permanent discoloration of the teeth yellow-gray-brown. This adverse reaction is more common during long term use of the drugs, but has been observed following repeated short term courses. Malformation of tooth enamel has also been reported. Tetracycline, therefore, should not be used in this age group unless other drugs are not likely to be effective or are contraindicated."

Whether this warning has done much good is hard to tell, since doctors very seldom read package inserts on drugs. Even if they do, warnings do not usually stop them from using the drugs when they feel like it. Particularly when the warning on the insert, like the one for tetracycline, doesn't really make it clear enough that these drugs carry side effects which merit their use *only* in critical situations.

One of those risks is even more grim than that of the side effects: superinfections. When an antibiotic fights one infection, it may encourage an even worse infection by a strain of bacteria that is resistant to the drug. Bacteria are remarkably adaptable organisms. Subsequent generations can develop resistance to a drug as their ancestors are exposed more and more. Penicillin in moderate doses once easily cured gonorrhea. Now it takes two *large* shots of the antibiotic to treat it, and it's sometimes necessary to use *additional* drugs! Two new strains of gonorrhea recently were discovered in the Philippines and in West Africa—strains which totally destroy penicillin's effectiveness.

Of course, Modern Medicine has a stronger drug ready for the stronger gonorrhea bacteria—spectinomycin. Spectinomycin costs six times as much and has even more side effects. Meanwhile, the gonorrhea bacteria have developed a strain which is resistant to spectinomycin, too! As the battle escalates, the germs grow stronger while the patients and their pocketbooks grow weaker.

All of which would not happen if doctors recognized that antibiotics have a place in the practice of medicine—a severely limited place—and if they *enforced* that restriction. A person may need penicillin or some other antibiotic three or four times during his or her entire life, at times when the stakes are worth the risks.

Unfortunately, doctors have seeded the entire population with these powerful drugs. Every year, from 8 to 10 million Americans go to the doctor when they have a cold. About ninety-five percent of them come away with a prescription—half of which are for antibiotics. Not only are these people duped into paying for something which has no effectiveness against their problem, but they're set up for the hazards of side effects and the risks of deadlier infections.

The doctor, once the agent of cure, has become the agent of disease. By *going too far* and diffusing the power of the extreme on the mean, Modern Medicine has weakened and corrupted even the management of extreme cases. The miracle I and other doctors were once proud to take part in has become a miracle of mayhem.

In 1890, Dr. Robert Koch derived a substance from tuberculosis bacteria which he claimed would cure the disease. When he injected it into patients, however, they got worse or died. In 1928, a drug called thorotrast was first used to aid in obtaining x-ray outlines of the liver, spleen, lymph nodes, and other organs. It took nineteen years to discover that even small doses of the drug caused cancer. In 1937, children who received a new antibacterial drug died because the drug was contaminated with a toxic chemical. In 1955, more than 100 fatal and near fatal cases of polio developed among unsuspecting people receiving certain lots of the Salk vaccine which contained presumably *inactivated* polio viruses. In 1959, about 500 children in Germany and 1,000 elsewhere were born severely deformed because their mothers had taken thalidomide, a sleeping pill and tranquilizer, during the early weeks of pregnancy. In 1962, a cholesterol-lowering drug, triparanol, was removed from the market when it was acknowledged that the drug caused numerous side effects, cataracts among them.

Most of these pharmaceutical backfires were corrected either when the drug was removed from the market or when the manufacturing error was discovered and tighter controls were established. The controls haven't been tight enough, though, because drug disasters like these are going on every day. Actually, the only apparatus that has grown stronger seems to be the machinery of keeping dangerous drugs moving from the factories through the hands of doctors into the mouths and bodies of unwary patients. Reserpine, a drug used against high blood pressure, is still prescribed, even though it was discovered in studies five years ago to triple the risk of breast cancer. Although insulin is turning up in scientific studies as one of the causes of diabetic blindness, its use is still heralded as a medical miracle.

Of course, if drugs were merely products of medical *science*, dealing with them would be a matter of science, rationality, and common sense. But drugs aren't merely scientific—they're *sacred*. Like the communion wafer which Catholics receive on the tongue, drugs are the communion wafers of Modern Medicine. When you take a drug, you're communing with one of the mysteries of the Church: the fact that the doctor can alter your inward and outward state if you have the faith to take the drug. And just as an undeniable factor in the healing or the spiritual boost the communicant gets at the altar rail is psychologically determined, the placebo effect—the power of suggestion—plays a tremendous role in whatever good a drug may do. As a matter of fact, there are some drugs and other procedures in which we know the placebo effect is the *primary* therapeutic agent!

The sacraments of the Catholic Church—or any other real church—seldom harm anyone. Doctor-prescribed sacramental drugs of Modern Medicine kill more people than illegal street drugs. A nationwide survey of medical examiners reported that street drugs cause twenty-six percent of drug *abuse* deaths. Valium and barbiturates—prescription drugs—made up another twenty-three percent of drug abuse deaths. This study did not take into account the 20,000 to 30,000 yearly deaths attributed to adverse reactions to drugs prescribed by doctors. The reason for the wide girth between the estimates is that doctors often fudge in stating whether or not drugs are the actual cause of death. If a patient has a terminal illness and dies during the drug therapy, the death will be attributed to the disease, even if the patient wouldn't normally have died for some time yet. The Boston Collaborative Drug Surveillance Program monitored patients admitted to acute disease medical wards and found the risk of being killed by drug therapy was better than one in 1,000 in American hospitals. An earlier survey by the same group found that the risk among hospitalized patients with serious chronic diseases such as cancer, heart disease, and alcoholic cirrhosis was four in 1,000. Of course, many of these people were in the hospital in the first place because of the effects of drugs prescribed by their doctors. Conservative estimates say that five percent of the people in American and British hospitals are there because of adverse reactions to drugs. Another conservative estimate puts the price tag on this preventable suffering at more than $3 billion.

Another, even more powerful, group of drugs whose use for the treatment of extreme conditions has shifted to common conditions is the steroid drugs. Steroids mimic the action of the adrenal glands, the most powerful regulators of body metabolism. Practically every organ is directly or indirectly affected by the secretions of the adrenal glands—as well as by the synthetic chemicals prescribed by the doctor. Once upon a time, steroid drugs were prescribed for severe adrenal insufficiency, for disturbances of the pituitary gland, and for certain life-threatening conditions such as lupus erythematosus, ulcerative colitis, leprosy, leukemia, Hodgkin's Disease, and lymphoma. Today, steroids are prescribed for conditions as common as sunburn, mononucleosis, acne, and a large variety of skin rashes which are often incorrectly diagnosed.

The entire list of precautions and adverse reactions to Prednisone fills two columns of small print in the *Physicians' Desk Reference,* the encyclopedia or "bible" of licensed drugs in the United States. Among the adverse reactions are: hypertension, loss of muscle tone, peptic ulcer with possible perforation and hemorrhage, impaired wound healing, increased sweating, convulsions, vertigo, menstrual irregularities, suppression of growth in children, manifestation of latent diabetes, psychic disturbances, and glaucoma. Is getting rid of some minor skin rash worth risking one of these disasters? Apparently some doctors think it is.

For example, a woman from Atlanta wrote me about her twenty-year-old daughter who had *never* had a menstrual period. At the age of eleven, the girl had developed a rash on her feet. The dermatologist prescribed Prednisone, and the youngster took it for three years. "Can anything be done for our daughter?" the woman asked me. "If only that dermatologist had told us that drug might do this to our daughter's reproductive system, we would have let her keep the rash!"

A young woman from Ohio wrote me that she had gotten a prescription for Prednisone accompanied by shots of another steroid, Kenalog, for poison ivy. "I suffered severe headaches, muscle cramps, swelling of my breasts, and bleeding for twenty-five days."

Her gynecologist told her the bleeding was caused by the medications she took for the poison ivy, so she must now undergo a D&C (scraping of the walls of the uterus).

A couple of years ago, the University of Chicago was slapped with a $77-million class-action suit filed on behalf of more than 1,000 women who unwittingly took part in a University experiment, some twenty-five years ago, with the synthetic hormone DES. This suit has special significance to me since I was then a student at the university's school of medicine and spent part of my time at Chicago Lying-In Hospital. I knew of the experiment, which tested the use of diethylstilbesterol in preventing threatened miscarriages. Being a conscientious medical student who trusted his school and believed his professors knew what they were doing, I didn't even question the experiment.

Of course neither I nor the 1,000 or so women should have trusted the school, because the professors *didn't* know what they were doing. In 1971, Dr. Arthur L. Herbst, then of Harvard Medical School, first announced that an alarmingly high rate of daughters of women who had taken DES were developing vaginal cancer. Later on we learned that male offspring of these women had an alarmingly high rate of genital malformations. And a statistically significant number of the women themselves were dying of cancer.

Of course, by then the bloom was off the rose as far as my unquestioning acceptance of medical science was concerned. I was not surprised when I heard the news. The damaging effects of hormones used in the Pill and in sex hormones used for menopause had already surfaced. If it hadn't been obvious twenty-five years ago that DES would have a damaging effect on the developing, vulnerable fetus, it was now.

Today, my surprise quotient is so low that I scarcely raise an eyebrow when I see that the same Dr. Herbst who unveiled the dangers in the first place has since come out with a paper that *plays down* the DES cancer risk! Since the damage has already been done and doctors have been exposed as ignorant of the possible dangers of the drugs they use, all that can be done now is retreat into the sacred language and make it look like the mistake wasn't a mistake at all, the danger not a danger at all. Try to convince the mothers who found out they were guinea pigs in the DES experiment. Try to convince their children. For every one of those diseased or deformed children, the risk has been 100 percent.

Dr. Herbst's own records show 300 cases of vaginal or cervical cancer in babies whose mothers were treated with DES. Imagine what a commotion Modern Medicine would have made a couple of years ago if "only 300 cases" of swine flu had been discovered. Would doctors *then* talk about how really miniscule the risk was? How about when a doctor wants to use antibiotics on an infant when the chances the child really needs them are less than one in 100,000?

DES is just *one* of the sex hormones prescribed for women at all stages of their lives. Tens of millions of women take such hormones daily in the form of contraceptive pills or menopausal estrogens. DES is still being given as the "morning after" contraceptive pill and to dry up breast milk. In 1975, the FDA sent a warning bulletin to doctors recommending that they switch women over age forty to a contraceptive other than the Pill. In 1977, the FDA required a warning brochure emphasizing the astronomical risk of cardiovascular disease among women over forty taking the Pill. Whether these warnings will do much good remains to be seen. Women over forty are still taking the Pill, either because they are not properly informed or because they choose to accept the risks. The overwhelming majority of women on the Pill are *under* forty. The risks are great for these women, too, and they include not only cardiovascular disease, but liver tumors, headaches, depression, and cancer. While taking the Pill over age forty multiplies the risk of dying from a heart attack by a factor of five, from age thirty to forty the Pill multiplies it by a factor of three. All women taking the Pill run a risk of high blood pressure six times greater than women not taking it. Their risk of stroke is four times greater, and their risk of thromboembolism is more than five times greater.

Doctors maintain the enormous market for the Pill by telling women it's safer to take the Pill than to get pregnant. Of course, that argument defies logic as well as science. First of all, the dangers of the Pill are just beginning to surface. They are the dangers of an unnatural substance interfering with body processes. Pregnancy, however, is a natural process, which the body is prepared to deal with—unless it is unhealthy in some way. To take the Pill is to *introduce* disease into the body. Comparing the risks of pregnancy to the risks of taking the Pill illogically jumbles together rich women, poor women, healthy women, sick women, women on the Pill, women off the Pill, women using other contraceptives, women using no contraceptives, married women, single women, teenagers, adults, promiscuous women, and non-promiscuous women. When these women get pregnant, they already bring to the statistics risk factors which have nothing to do with pregnancy.

Of course, it's bad science to compare the Pill's dangers with pregnancy anyway. The real question is: Is the Pill safer than other forms of contraception?

Added to the 10 million women who still take the Pill are more than 5 million who take menopausal estrogens. Again, these drugs have been implicated so strongly in the causation of gall bladder disease and cancer of the uterus (they multiply the risk by a factor of five to twelve) that the FDA has been forced to issue warnings to doctors and patients. Warnings which have gone largely unheeded, as far as doctors are concerned. For instead of limiting the use of these drugs to infrequent, short term relief of severe symptoms, most doctors use them *routinely* supposedly to *prevent* the mildest of menopausal discomforts. Estrogen therapy is used to preserve youth, for cosmetic purposes, to relieve depression, and for the prevention of cardiovascular disease—all for which its effectiveness has been disproved. Estrogens also are used to prevent bone demineralization in older women. Exercise and diet also can prevent demineralization—and they don't cause cancer. Many women obtain estrogens from their doctor at the first sign of depression during middle age. Seldom does the doctor take the time to find out if perhaps the depression isn't caused by some other factor, something that can be treated without estrogen or—perish the thought—without *any* drug.

Actually, quite a few drugs are invented and prescribed for conditions which can be treated perfectly well with less dangerous methods. Antihypertension drugs have filled such a market void for an easy way to lower blood pressure that their popularity has soared in the few years they've been available. Now a doctor no longer has to tell a person with high blood pressure that his lifestyle is killing him. He can just write a prescription for a drug and use his powers of persuasion to get the patient to take the drug. We even have television, radio, and magazine commercials urging people to take their high blood pressure medication! Somehow, somewhere, someone has convinced enough people that taking these drugs is the only way to lower blood pressure. And someone has, of course, also failed to alert a lot of people to the side effects of these drugs. Someone is aware of those side effects, though, because many of the high blood pressure drug ads in the medical journals are for drugs designed to deal with the side effects of the antihypertension drugs!

Some of those side effects include: rash, hives, sensitivity to light, dizziness, weakness, muscle cramps, inflammation of the blood vessels, tingling sensation in the skin, joint aches, confusion, difficulty concentrating, muscle spasms, nausea, and loss of sex drive and potency. That last side effect, by the way, affects both men *and* women on antihypertensives. Sometimes I wonder just how much of the middle aged population suffers from impotence—not from any psychological cause but simply from their blood pressure medication. All the sex therapy in the world won't correct drug-induced impotence and loss of libido. If doctors aren't aware of the side effects from these drugs, they aren't doing their job, because the manufacturers list them in the *Physicians' Desk Reference (PDR)*. If they do know about them and prescribe these drugs anyway, you have to stop and wonder: would a doctor who was found to have high blood pressure take these drugs *himself?*

Perhaps any doctor foolish enough to prescribe these drugs is also foolish enough to take them himself, since most doctors are aware of the controversy over whether these drugs do any good *at all.* Even if you assume that high blood pressure is dangerous, doctors are still guilty of being a bit quick with the prescription. Many people who receive high blood pressure medication are really borderline cases:

their blood pressure isn't high enough to warrant a drug with the side effects of antihypertensives. Most of these people could more effectively lower their blood pressure through relaxation therapy, dietary or lifestyle changes. In one study, relaxation therapy reduced blood pressure faster and farther than drug therapy. Similar studies have shown that weight loss, reduction of salt intake, vegetarian diet, and exercise can also lower blood pressure at least as effectively and certainly more safely than drug therapy. There's little doubt that many patients don't need to lower their blood pressure at all, since as soon as they leave the danger zone of the doctor's office, their blood pressure returns to normal.

One of the unwritten rules in Modern Medicine is always to write a prescription for a new drug quickly, before all its side effects have come to the surface. Nowhere is this syndrome more evident than in the unleashing of the herd of new antiarthritic drugs on the unsuspecting patients. Nowhere is it more evident that the "cures" are worse than the disease.

Within the last few years, a torrent of advertisements in medical journals has heralded the coming of such anti-arthritis drugs as Butazolidin alka, Motrin, Indocin, Naprosyn, Nalfon, Tolectin, and others. The drug companies have spared neither time nor money in rushing their arthritis "cures" to the marketplace. Millions upon millions of prescriptions have been written. And in just these few years, this new class of drugs has a record of side effects that promises to rival antibiotics and hormones as genuine public health menaces.

Just *reading* the information supplied *by the manufacturer* of Butazolidin alka, and thinking that your doctor actually is prescribing the stuff to you is enough to make you ill: "This is a potent drug; its misuse can lead to serious results. Cases of leukemia have been reported in patients with a history of short and long term therapy. The majority of the patients were over forty." If you read further you find that your doctor is setting you up for a possible 92 adverse reactions, including headaches, vertigo, coma, hypertension, retinal hemorrhage, and hepatitis. The company goes on to admit: "Carefully instruct and observe the individual patient, especially the aging (forty and over) who have increased susceptibility to the drug. Use lowest effective dosage. Weigh initially unpredictable benefits against risk of severe, even fatal reactions. The disease condition itself is unaltered by the drug."

After reading that, you have to wonder why the drug company would bother marketing the stuff. What doctor would give such poison to his patient? What person would willingly take this drug? You can stop wondering, because Butazolidin alka makes millions of dollars for its manufacturer. Doctors may or may not be aware of the drug's disastrous side effects. They may not be offended by the admission by the company that the doctor has to weigh *unpredictable* benefits against the possibility of *death*. They just may not care.

Or they may be guided by a force that goes beyond logic and consideration—the rhythm of a religious sacrifice.

In the case of at least one antiarthritis drug, Naprosyn, the sacrifice has graduated into a *farce*. Though the FDA has discovered that Syntex, the drug's manufacturer, falsified records of tumors and animal deaths during the safety tests for its drug, the government is unable to remove the drug from the market without long and tedious proceedings.

No modern medical procedure better displays the inquisitorial nature of Modern Medicine than the drugging of so called "hyperactive" children. Originally, behavior controlling drugs were used to treat only the most severe cases of mental illness. But today, drugs such as Dexedrine, Cylert, Ritalin, and Tofranil are being used on more than a million children throughout the United States—on the basis of often flimsy diagnostic criteria of hyperactivity and minimal brain damage. Some medical tests, when performed correctly, are conclusive. But there is no single diagnostic test that will identify a child as hyperactive or any of the twenty-one other names assigned to this syndrome. The list of inconclusive tests is at least as long as the list of names. All a doctor has to go on is a list of inconclusive tests and the "educated" guess of an "expert."

One school in Texas took advantage of this ambiguity and diagnosed forty percent of its students as minimally brain damaged in a year when government money was available to treat that syndrome.

Two years later, this money was no longer available, but funds for treating children with language learning disabilities were floating around. Suddenly, the minimally brain damaged students disappeared and thirty-five percent of the children were diagnosed as having language learning disabilities!

If that school district and others took the government money and used it on teachers' salaries, books, playground equipment, and supplies, their larceny could be forgiven. But what happens is that the child who can't sit still in class—instead of being given tasks that will interest and occupy him—is diagnosed as hyperactive and "managed" by drugs. These drugs are not without serious side effects. Not only do they suppress growth and cause high blood pressure, nervousness, and insomnia, but they transform children into "brave new world" type zombies. Sure, the kids slow down—dramatically. They're also less responsive and enthusiastic, and more humorless and apathetic. And they don't perform any better when measured objectively over long periods of time.

The original authors of scientific studies on these behavior modifying drugs have tried to disassociate themselves from their present use by claiming that the problem isn't the drugs' existence but the way doctors over-diagnose, mis-diagnose, and overmedicate. While such arguments may salvage a few individual reputations, keep in mind that the original investigators and authors have made little or no attempt to properly limit the use of their discoveries. On the contrary, we still have three-page ads in the medical journals which picture a school teacher proudly proclaiming, "How wonderful! Andy's handwriting no longer looks like hen scratchings." This is the first time in history that powerful drugs have been sold to cure poor penmanship! And sold quite successfully, I might add. More than a million children are being given these drugs, a yearly habit that stuffs tens of millions of dollars into the pockets of the drug companies.

Nowhere does the Church's Inquisition emerge as clearly as it does through the drugging of children as a means of control. The medieval Inquisition went beyond defining unorthodox beliefs and behavior as a "sin" and started calling them a crime. Criminals were punished, first by the Church and then by the secular authorities. Modern Medicine sets up its Inquisition to define behavior which doesn't conform as *sick*. Then it proceeds to "punish" the guilty by "managing" them with drugs. Since the primary purpose of schools is not to liberate the intelligence through learning but to create properly socialized and manageable citizens, the Medical Church and the State join forces to maintain public order. The Church enforces the behavior standards that suit the State, and the State enforces the exclusive view of reality that allows the Church to flourish. All in the name of Health—which, in reality, is not even a minor consideration of either party.

Witness the vigor with which the State proselytizes Modern Medicine's line of Holy Waters. Now, Holy Waters are special cases slightly removed from drugs in that the thin veil of diagnostic necessity has been removed. *Everybody* needs—and gets—the Holy Waters: routine silver nitrate in the eyes of the newborn, routine intravenous fluids to laboring mothers and other hospital patients, routine immunizations, and fluoridation of water supplies. All four of these procedures are automatically, thoughtlessly imposed on people whether they wish them or not, whether they need them or not. All four of them are at best unnecessary ninety-nine percent of the time. All four of them are of questionable safety. Yet all of them—except the intravenous fluids so far—are not only Church Law, but State Law as well.

I'll never forget the overwhelming compulsion of the priest making his way to the premature nursery to get some holy water on the infants and baptize them before they died. That same fierce compulsion motivates the priests of Modern Medicine in slapping their Holy Waters on their patients.

One of the mottoes medical students are taught to memorize but never practice—such as "first do no harm"—is "when you hear the sound of hoofbeats, think of horses before zebras." In other words, when symptoms present themselves, first consider the most obvious, common sense cause. As you can see, this motto doesn't survive very long in most doctors' practices. You can't use powerful and expensive drugs and procedures on horses. So what the doctor does is hear a herd of zebras every time, and treat accordingly. If a child is bored or can't sit still, he's hyperactive and needs a drug. If your joints are stiff because you don't exercise them the way you should, you need a drug. If your blood pressure is a little high, you need a drug. If you've got the sniffles, you need a drug. If your life isn't going the way it should, you need a drug. On and on ... the zebras keep coming.

One of the factors that keeps those zebras coming is the cozy and profitable relationship that exists between the drug companies and doctors. The drug companies spend an average of $6,000 per year on each and every doctor in the United States for the purpose of getting them to use their drugs. Company "detail" men, actually salesmen, build friendly, profitable relationships with the doctors on their route, wining and dining, doing favors, handing out samples of drugs. The sad fact is that most of the information reaching doctors about the uses and abuses of drugs comes from the drug companies, through the detail men and advertising in medical journals. Since most of the clinical test reports are financed by the drug companies, information from these, too, is highly suspect.

A commission of distinguished scientists, including four Nobel Laureates, studied the drug problem and found that the culprits are the doctors and the scientists who test the drugs. They found clinical trials of new drugs were "a shambles." The FDA spot checked the work of some doctors doing such clinical trials and found twenty percent guilty of a wide range of unethical practices, including giving incorrect dosages and falsifying records. In a third of the reports checked by the FDA, the trial had not been carried out at all. In another third, the experimental protocol was not followed. In only a third of the tests could the results be considered scientifically worthwhile! [*Journal of the American Medical Association,* November 3, 1975.]

Despite the obvious corruption of the drug company/doctor marketing connection, I don't blame the drug companies, the detail men, the government agencies which are supposed to police these activities, or the patients who badger their doctors for drugs. Doctors have enough facts in their possession to know what's going on. Even where the drug is fully tested and the side effects and limitations of the drug are well known, most of the harm is done by doctors indiscriminately prescribing the drug. Doctors, after all, are the ones who claim the sacred power and the ethical superiority that goes with it. The drug companies are in business to make money, and they do that by selling as much of their product as they can at as high a price as they can. And although the drug companies subvert the scientific process through which drugs are tested, certified, and made available to doctors, once the drugs are available, they *do* let doctors know—albeit subtly—just what these drugs can and cannot do.

The drug companies *don't have* to fight against package inserts that would explain the side effects and hazards of medications to the people who take them: the American Medical Association does it for them. Doctors either play down the side effects or conceal them altogether on the grounds that the doctor-patient relationship would be endangered. "If I had to explain things to patients, I could never get through my office hours." Or, "If patients knew everything these drugs could do, they never would take them." Rather than protecting the patient, the doctor protects the sacred relationship—which relies on ignorance to survive. Blind faith.

If doctors still obeyed the first rule of medicine—*Primum, non nocere,* first do no harm—there would be no need for them to enforce the blind faith of their patients. When it came down to weighing risks against benefits, the patient's welfare would be the first consideration. But that rule has been rationalized into a grotesque mutation that allows the doctor to weigh risks and benefits in a totally different ethical frame. Now the rule is First Do *Something.* Now, you hurt the patients most by *not* giving them something, whether it's a drug or some other procedure. Whether the "something" does any good or not is irrelevant. (To *question* it is irreverent!) Whether it does any harm matters even less. If the treatment does happen to hurt enough to make the patient complain, the doctor merely says "Learn to live with it."

Of course, a doctor would never consider saying that to a patient until he had tried at least one drug. Doctors have completely bought the advertising slogan "Better Living Through Chemistry." You might think the reason for this is purely economic. The doctor can write a prescription in a few seconds, whereas discussing with the patient the state of his nutrition, exercise patterns, career, and psyche would certainly take up more time and allow him to see fewer patients. In a fee-for-service system, the quick chemical fix has its obvious financial reward for the doctor as well as for the pharmacist and the drug manufacturer.

I think the reasons go deeper than money. One way to look at it—though an admittedly cynical way—is to recognize that doctors have throughout the ages embraced the wrong ideas. Considering the drug problem in our time, the adamant disregard of sterility in the nineteenth century, leeches, bleeding, purgatives, you could make a case that medicine has always been hazardous to the majority of patients.

That—and most doctors' high regard for financial reward—helps explain what the patient is up against. If you go deeper still, you come up against philosophical reasons that I can only describe as the Theology of Modern Medicine. Ironically, this theology is a corruption of certain aspects of Christian theology.

If you look at almost any other system of medicine besides the Western, you'll find a heavy reliance on food. The "food" of Modern Medicine, however, is the drug. The American doctor, aside from a very fragmentary and usually incorrect approach to certain "therapeutic diets" (gout, diabetic, low salt, gallbladder, weight reduction, low cholesterol), completely disregards nutrition. Those who are concerned with nutrition are labeled faddists, freaks, extremists, radicals, and quacks. Occasionally, they're (more correctly) referred to as *heretics*.

Oriental medicine, on the other hand, recognizes and utilizes the importance of nutrition in health. If you look at Oriental religion, you'll find that it, too, regards food as important to a person's spiritual welfare. But Western religion, namely Christianity, did exactly what Modern Medicine did: substituted as an object of reverence a sacramental, symbolic food in place of real food. "What goes into the mouth does not make a man unclean; it is what comes out of the mouth that makes him unclean." (Matthew 15:11)

Perhaps in their zeal to reject the Old Testament dietary laws, some of the early Christian leaders moved too far in the opposite direction and bypassed nutrition altogether. There's no doubt that Modern Medicine took the hint and carried it to extremes. Obviously, as far as a person's health is concerned, what goes into the mouth is at least as important as what comes out. In fact, what goes in may *determine* what comes out. Yet if anyone dares to claim that a person *is* what he or she eats, Modern Medicine regards them as a heretic or an intellectual weakling. Instead, the "food" with the sacred "power" is the drug, the man-made chemical coursing through your veins, for better or for worse.

To protect yourself from the pusher-priest, you again have to make the heretic's radical leap of unfaith. Don't trust your doctor. Assume that if he prescribes a drug, it's dangerous. There is no safe drug. Eli Lilly himself once said that a drug without toxic effects is no drug at all. *Every* drug has to be approached with suspicion.

That goes double if you're pregnant. In fact, if you're pregnant, you and your baby are better off if you stay away from all drugs *completely*. A drug that has minor side effects or even no side effects *on you* may do irreparable harm to a developing fetus. Hundreds of drugs are marketed long before their effects on the fetus are known. Unless you want to donate your baby's welfare to science and be one of the first to find out a drug's effects, don't take *any* drug unless your life is at stake.

That includes aspirin. Though it's been around for eighty or more years, doctors still don't know how aspirin works. Because it's been a "friend of the family" for so long, people don't realize that aspirin is not without side effects and dangers of its own. Besides the most common side effect, stomach bleeding, aspirin can cause a hemorrhage under the scalp of a newborn if a mother takes it within seventy-two hours of delivery. I've often wondered why doctors always say to take "two tablets" of five grains each despite the availability of a single, ten-grain aspirin tablet. Could there be some sort of religious significance in receiving ten of something in two tablets?

Before you take the *first dose* of any medication your doctor prescribes, you should make it your business to find out more about the drug than the doctor himself knows. Again, learning more about your situation than the doctor won't be all that difficult. Doctors get most of their information about drugs from advertisements and from detail men and their pamphlet handouts. All you have to do is spend some time with a good book or two in order to get the information you need before deciding whether to take a drug or not.

The best book to start with is the *Physicians' Desk Reference,* the *PDR.* The *PDR* is the beginning of knowledge about drugs. Although it's easily available now, up until about two years ago the publisher refused to distribute it to other than members of the medical profession. I wasn't aware of this when I gave the *PDR* many plugs in my column and newsletter. Finally, I got a letter from the publisher telling me to please stop referring people to their book since they distributed it only to professionals. They felt that the public wouldn't understand the *PDR* and would be confused by it. Well, I published that letter in my column and I commented that it was the first time in history a publisher didn't want to sell his books. Shortly thereafter, without any kind of fanfare, the *PDR* not only started showing up in bookstores, but it was *promoted* in bookstores! Now, if you go into the bookstores, you'll see *piles* of *PDR*'s. I guess the publisher finally got the idea.

Of course, you don't have to buy the book. Almost every public library now has it. You shouldn't worry about understanding it. Anybody with an eighth grade education and a dictionary can read *any* medical book. Even doctors will testify that patients always seem to be able to pick out and understand the parts that they *must* know.

The *PDR* is good because all the information is provided by the drug companies in an effort to *protect themselves.* Not only does the FDA require them to put in all the information they have, but they also want to ward off any liability claims against them. In effect, they are saying to the doctor: we are telling you everything we know about this drug. What it may be useful for. What it may do to the person who takes it. The wonderful thing that seems to be happening is that the *PDR* is becoming more and more discreet. For example, the latest issues divide drug side effects into major categories according to how frequently they can occur. Now at least you've got horse race odds when you take your medicine.

The *PDR* can be considered the "bible" of the Church of Modern Medicine, especially since for a long time it was forbidden literature except to the priesthood. But there are other sources for the kind of drug information you need. The American Medical Association publishes a *Drug Evaluations* book which in some cases gives even more information than the *PDR*. For one thing, the AMA book has a list of cross-referenced symptoms in the back. You look up your symptom or your side effect and it will tell you which drugs are indicated or suspected.

Because we're living in an era of poly-pharmacy—everybody is taking more than one drug at a time—you've got to become aware of the dangers of *combinations of drugs*. One drug may have side effects harmful to one organ three or four percent of the time, two percent to another organ, six percent to another. A second drug may have dangers for one organ that occur three percent, dangers for another organ ten percent. If you're taking enough drugs, the danger can easily add up to more than 100 percent. You're virtually *assured* of suffering some toxic effect! Even more dangerous are the *potentiating* effects of drug combinations. One drug might have only a five percent chance of hurting you. But in combination with another drug, the danger can be *multiplied* by a factor of two, three, four, five . . . who knows? Not only can the risk be multiplied, but so can the *strength* of the toxic effect! There are books which give lists of drugs which interact with a given drug. (An excellent one which I use is Eric Martin's *Hazards of Medications*.) Of course, you also should let your doctor know what drugs you are taking. But *don't* rely on his knowledge of any dangerous cross-reactions that might occur.

You should be aware of all the drugs for which the side effects are the same as the indications. This isn't as rare as you might think. For example, if you read the list of indications for Valium, and then read the list of side effects, you'll find that the lists are more or less interchangeable! Under the indications you'll find: anxiety, fatigue, depression, acute agitation, tremors, hallucinosis, skeletal muscle spasms. And under the side effects: anxiety, fatigue, depression, acute hyperexcited states, tremors, hallucinations, increased muscle spasticity! I admit I don't know how to use a drug like this: what am I supposed to do if I prescribe it and the symptoms continue? Stop the drug or double the dose? What strategy lies behind using drugs like this is a mystery to me. Perhaps doctors are playing the placebo effect for all it's worth? Or maybe they are merely trying to *sanctify* a patient's original symptoms by giving a drug that *causes* them? Maybe they figure the symptoms will go away when the drug is withdrawn, in the fashion of primitive rites of purification and purging? In any case, Valium is the largest selling drug in history, with prescriptions approaching 60 million a year. Maybe it *deserves* to be the largest selling drug in history, since, by having identical indications and side effects, it achieves what all systems of science, art, and faith strive for: *Unity!*

You should not let your doctor prescribe a drug without asking him lots of questions. Ask him what will happen if you don't take the drug. Ask him what the drug is supposed to do for you and *how* it's going to do it. You can also ask him the same questions you will bring to the *PDR*, questions about side effects and situations when the drug is not advised. Don't expect too explicit an answer. Most drugs' mechanisms remain mysteries even to the people who develop them.

Once you've exposed yourself to all this information, you have to sit down and decide whether or not you want to take the drug. Again, don't trust your doctor's decision. Even if you can get him to admit to the side effects, he'll most likely discount them by saying they occur only in a small percentage of cases. You also might get that impression from the *PDR* or any other book you consult. Don't be misled by risks that are expressed in small percentages. If you judge the danger of an iceberg by the size of the part that's above the water, you're not going to stay afloat very long. Like a game of Russian Roulette, for the person who gets the loaded chamber, the risk is 100 percent. But *unlike* that game, for the person taking a drug *no chamber is entirely empty.* Every drug stresses and hurts your body in some way.

The doctor doesn't consider this because his philosophy of decision is corrupted. *First Do Something.* The doctor is going to find himself saying ridiculous things such as, "The Pill is safer than pregnancy." Because the doctor *believes* it, he's dangerous. You have to determine your risk individually. Only you, as you read up on the drug, will be able to recognize certain conditions you have or have had which might make the drug even more dangerous. And only you will be able to decide whether or not you want to risk going through one or more of whatever side effects you find there in exchange for the *possible* benefit the drug may deliver.

Most of all, you should keep in mind that you can *refuse* to take the drug. It's *your* health that's at stake. If you read things that make you not want to take the drug, first of all confront the doctor with the information. Through cajolery, badgering, or some process of persuasion, you should convince the doctor that you really want to avoid the drug. As in all confrontations with doctors, his reaction may tell you more than you bargained for. You may once and for all recognize that his opinion is no more valid than yours.

On the other hand, if you don't find anything in your research to dissuade you from taking the drug, if the possible benefits appear to outweigh the risks, you're still not home free. You still have to protect yourself. First of all, make sure you carry out the instructions given by your doctor. If you find his instructions are different from the prescribing information in the *PDR*, you should ask him why. He may have a perfectly good reason: his experience may suggest that the drug works best when taken according to his instructions. Or he may be making a mistake that could decide whether or not the drug will help you or hurt you.

Another reason why you should follow the instructions is that often these will include various tests that should be carried out while you're taking the drug, tests that are designed to reveal any serious adverse effects before they go too far. These tests are usually found with the prescribing information. Every doctor knows about or has access to this information. Yet few doctors bother to fulfill this responsibility. So it's up to you to make sure your body's reaction to the drug is tested.

You should also monitor the drug's effect subjectively. How does the drug make you feel? If you experience any side effects—no matter how unimportant they may seem at first—you should call your doctor and let him know. Here is where your homework can really pay off, because your doctor may not be aware of certain side effects that are a signal to stop taking the drug. On the other hand, some side effects are temporary, and if you've already made up your mind to take the drug, you may not want to stop as long as the discomfort is temporary. If you're hit by a serious side effect, you should immediately seek medical attention. Don't wait too long for your doctor to get in touch with you. Go to the hospital emergency room. You're not only protecting your health, but you're covering all the bases in the event any legal action ever results from the therapy.

If on the basis of your complaints of side effects, or because you refuse to take a certain drug at all, your doctor prescribes *another* drug, make sure it's not the *same substance* with a different brand name. The doctor may himself be ignorant—or he may be trying to put one over on you.

If you find yourself having to protect your child from the recommendations of school officials and doctors that he or she be "treated" for hyperactivity, your first move should be to prepare yourself to start with simple measures but be willing and able to go on to more drastic maneuvers. The simplest procedure involves a little diplomacy, a little skillful deception of professionals, and perhaps a few changes in how you manage your child. Have a conference with the classroom teacher. Let him or her know that you don't want your child receiving drugs and that you want to explore alternative ways of dealing with the problem. It helps to try to find out exactly what aspects of your child's behavior led the teacher to label him or her "hyperactive." You can ask for suggestions on how to change your management of the child at home in order to better prepare for the classroom. Here is where you've got to be ready to lie a little. You should give the teacher's suggestions honest consideration. If they sound reasonable, you should consider changes. But if they don't seem like things you could do without sacrificing family habits and practices that you consider important, you should discard them. You don't have to tell the teacher that. You can lie and rave about how your child has changed so positively since you tried his or her suggestions. Chances are that will end the problem, since the teacher's expectations of the child's behavior determine the teacher's perception of it, and may even determine the child's actual behavior in accord with the self-fulfilling prophecy.

The next step is to have a conference with the teacher to explore possible ways in which the classroom management could be modified. You're going to meet resistance here, because the philosophy of most schools—despite all the lip service to individual attention and consideration—is that the student has to fit the mold cast by the school.

At this point, if you're not getting anywhere, you might want to consult with people who have wisdom and whom you trust. These can be special education experts or grandmothers.

Consider a change in your child's classroom. Before you allow a doctor to tamper with your child's chemistry, you should realize that perhaps it's the "chemistry" between child and teacher, or child and classmates, that is really at fault. A move to another school could be the answer for the same reasons.

The most drastic solution is to remove your child from school altogether and have him or her tutored at home, if state law permits.

If your child really does seem to have a behavior problem that goes beyond the normal range of childhood intractability, you might want to consider a solution many families have successfully tried: the Feingold diet. Dr. Ben Feingold is the chief of the Kaiser Foundation's allergy clinics. His diet eliminates food coloring and other artificial additives, and certain natural foods—on the assumption that certain substances in these foods stimulate a child who is especially susceptible. The concept is sound—although vigorously attacked by advocates of drug therapy.

You can't rely on your doctor to aid you in your struggle to keep a child diagnosed as hyperactive off drugs. The doctor may play along with you and say, "Well, let's talk to the teacher and try to change the environment," but in ninety-nine out of one hundred cases the doctor will return to the drugs. The same is likely to happen if you try to get your doctor to treat you without drugs in any other situation. Doctors simply don't believe in non-drug therapies. For one thing, very few of them *know how* to treat without drugs. So they don't believe in it. If you have high blood pressure and your doctor wants to put you on drugs but you don't want to take them, he might try by having you lose weight and by exercising. But he'll make only a half-hearted attempt because in the first place he doesn't believe in it and in the second place doctors don't know enough about nutrition and lifestyle to really show a patient how to make a useful change. Maybe one doctor in fifty knows.

From the standpoint of the patient, of course, it makes perfectly good sense to want to be treated without drugs. But from the standpoint of the doctor, it's totally outrageous. Again, the ethics of the doctor and the ethics of the patient conflict. That shouldn't come as too big a surprise. Medical ethics are usually the opposite of traditional ethics. For instance, if you're in the operating room and somebody finds a sponge in the belly left from a previous operation, traditional ethics would make sure that somebody in the family found out about it. Medical ethics tells you to keep your mouth shut about it. The surgeon will say, "I don't want anybody to know about this," and if the nurse tells the family, she'll be out of a job. Medical ethics also waffles on the point of stopping at the scene of an accident. If a doctor passes the scene of an accident, traditional ethics tells him to stop and try to save a life. Medical ethics tells him first to find out if the state has a Good Samaritan law.

The ethics of Modern Medicine are different from traditional religious ethics as well as from traditional social ethics. Religious systems that are in conflict generally try to dissubstantiate the ethics and beliefs of the systems they are at odds with. In the Church of Modern Medicine, the doctor who treats without drugs is regarded as a heretic because he or she appears to have rejected the sacrament of medication. Non-drug healers are regarded as belonging to a different religious system and are thought of as quacks, nuts, or faddists. The religious restrictions are so stringent that doctors are discouraged from even *associating* with the infidels. The AMA code of ethics says that M.D.s are not supposed to associate with cultists. They're not to talk to them, not to have them in their homes! If you keep in mind that this is the type of person that's advising you to take this or that dangerous substance into your body, you should have no problem mustering the motivation to protect yourself.

3
Ritual Mutilations

I believe that my generation of doctors will be remembered for two things: the miracles that turned to mayhem, such as penicillin and cortisone, and for the millions of mutilations which are ceremoniously carried out every year in operating rooms.

Conservative estimates—such as that made by a congressional subcommittee—say that about 2.4 million operations performed every year are unnecessary, and that these operations cost $4 billion and 12,000 lives, or five percent of the quarter million deaths following or during surgery each year. The independent Health Research Group says the number of unnecessary operations is more than 3 million. And various studies have put the number of useless operations between eleven and thirty percent. My feeling is that somewhere around ninety percent of surgery is a waste of time, energy, money, and life.

One study, for example, closely reviewed people who were recommended for surgery. Not only did they find that most of them needed no surgery, but fully *half of them needed no medical treatment at all!* The formation of committees to review tissue removed in operations has resulted in some telling statistics. In one case, 262 appendectomies were performed the year *before* a tissue committee began overseeing surgery. During the first year of the committee's review, the number dropped to 178. Within a few years, the number dropped to 62. The percentage of normal appendices removed fell fifty-five percent. In another hospital, the number of appendectomies was slashed by two-thirds after a tissue committee went to work.

These committees and study teams are composed of doctors who are still working within the belief system of Modern Medicine. There are dozens of common operations they would no doubt see as useful most of the time, such as cancer surgery, coronary bypass surgery, and hysterectomies. Yet as far as I'm concerned, ninety percent of the most common operations, including these, are at best of little value and at worst quite harmful.

The victims of a lot of needless surgery are children. Tonsillectomy is one of the most common surgical procedures in the United States. Half of all pediatric surgery is for the removal of tonsils. About a million are done every year. Yet the operation has never been demonstrated to do very much good.

Back around the same time I got into trouble for cutting urological workups on children at an outpatient clinic, I got into trouble again for not discussing the size of tonsils. There are very rare cases—less than one in 1,000—where someone may need a tonsillectomy. I'm not talking about when the child snores or breathes noisily. But when it really impedes the child's breathing, if he or she is really choking, the tonsils may have to come out. You don't have to *ask* a child or a parent about it. It's obvious! So I cut out that question on the examination. Of course, the number of tonsillectomies went way down. As you might expect, I soon got a call from the chairman of the ear, nose, and throat department: I was threatening his teaching program.

Tonsillectomies have been performed for more than 2,000 years, and their usefulness in most cases never has been proved. Doctors still can't agree on when the operation should or shouldn't be performed. The best reason doctors and parents can give for the attack on the tonsils is, as if they were some mountain range that had to be conquered, "because they're there."

Parents are lulled into believing that the operation "can't do any harm." Though physical complications are rare, they're not altogether non-existent. Mortality ranges in different surveys from one in 3,000 to one in 10,000. Emotional complications abound. Getting to eat all the ice cream you want doesn't make up for the justified fear a child experiences that his parents and the doctor are ganging up on him. A lot of children show marked changes for the worse in their behavior after the operation. They're more depressed, pessimistic, afraid, and generally awkward in the family. Who can blame them? They can sense, and unfortunately be seriously affected by, a patently absurd—though dangerous—situation.

Women also seem to be the victims of a lot of unnecessary surgery. Another operation steadily climbing towards the million-a-year mark is the hysterectomy. The National Center for Health Statistics estimated that 690,000 women had their uteruses removed in 1973, which results in a rate of 647.7 per 100,000 females. Besides the fact that this is a higher rate than for any other operation, if the rate continued, it would mean that *half* of all women would lose their uterus by age 65! That's if the rate holds steady. Actually, it's *growing.* In 1975, 808,000 hysterectomies were performed.

Very few of them were necessary. In six New York hospitals, forty-three percent of the hysterectomies reviewed were found to be unjustified. Women with abnormal bleeding from the uterus and abnormally heavy menstrual blood flow were given hysterectomies even though other treatments—or no treatment at all—would have most likely worked just as well.

In their lusting after the status and power of surgeons, obstetricians are rapidly turning the natural process of childbirth into a surgical procedure. Layer upon layer of "treatment" buries the experience under the mantle of sickness, as each layer requires another layer to compensate for its adverse effects. Strangely enough, you can always count on doctors to take credit for the *compensations*, but not for the medical disasters that make the compensations necessary in the first place!

The first major intrusion into childbirth was the introduction of forceps. Two sinister sixteenth-century barber-surgeons, the Chamberlen brothers, always carried a huge wooden box into the delivery room. They sent everyone else out of the room and blindfolded the mother in labor before opening the box. It wasn't until the nineteenth century that the contents of the box became widely known: obstetrical forceps. Using forceps to extract the baby whether or not the birth proceeds normally was the first step towards turning labor and delivery into surgery.

The next step came as scientists became interested in the birthing process. Doctors began to compete with midwives, and as they won, the process came to be supervised by the male doctor rather than the female midwife. It wasn't long before childbirth moved from the home into the hospital, where all the trappings and stage settings for treating it as a disease could be easily arranged. Of course, when the male doctors took over childbirth, it *did* become a disease. The doctors did something the midwives never did: they went right from the autopsy labs where they were handling corpses to the maternity wards to attend births. Maternal and infant death rates skyrocketed far beyond where they had been when midwives delivered babies. One courageous doctor, Ignaz Philipp Semmelweis, pointed out the deadly connection and was hounded out of medicine and into an insane asylum for suggesting that doctors were the agents of disease. Once Semmelweis' suggestion that doctors wash their hands before attending a birth was adopted, maternal and infant mortality rates dropped—an event for which the profession predictably took credit.

Once it became possible to drug the mother into a state of helpless oblivion, the obstetrician could become even more powerful. Since the mother couldn't assist in the delivery while unconscious, the forceps' place in the delivery room was assured.

Sedated, feet in stirrups, shaven, attached to an intravenous fluid bag and a battery of monitors, the woman in labor is set up so well for surgery, an operation had to be *invented* so the scene wouldn't go to waste. Enter the episiotomy. So routine is this surgical slicing of the perineum to widen the opening of the vagina that few women and even fewer doctors think twice about it. Doctors claim that the surgical incision is straighter and simpler to repair than the tear that is likely to occur when the baby's head and shoulders are born. They fail to acknowledge that if the woman is not drugged silly, and if she's properly coached by someone who knows what's going on, and if she's prepared, then she will know how and when to push and not push to *ease* the baby out. When the birth is a conscious, deliberate experience, the perineal tear can usually be avoided. After all, the vagina was *made* to stretch and allow a baby to pass through. Even if tearing does occur, there's no evidence that the surgical incision heals better than a tear. Quite the contrary, my experience demonstrates that tears heal *better*, and with *less* discomfort, than episiotomies. There is some feeling that the episiotomy may lead to a later lessening of sexual pleasure.

Obstetricians were not long satisfied by the minor surgery of the episiotomy. They had to have something more awesome and dangerous. After all, the delivery room setting only adds to the feeling that something terribly abnormal must be happening here. And such an abnormal process surely demands medical intervention. The more extreme the better. And since the delivery room is really an operating room disguised by the simple addition of an incubator, what really should be going on here is a full blown operation. Hence the obstetrical sacrifice graduates beyond the simple mutilation of the episiotomy to the most sinister development of modern obstetrics, the epidemic of Caesarean deliveries.

Fetal monitoring—listening to the fetal heart either through the mother's abdomen or, most recently, through electrodes screwed into the infant's scalp during labor—is the diagnostic sowing procedure that is reaping the harvest of Caesarean section deliveries. Whether or not the fetus is really in trouble, if the monitor says something is wrong, there's a rush to slice the mother open and remove the baby. Then the obstetrician can bask in all the limelight that comes with performing a miracle. After all, he's snatched a life from the jaws of certain death or disablement. Studies of comparable deliveries show that Caesarean deliveries occur three to four times more often in births attended by electronic fetal monitoring than in those monitored with a stethoscope. That's not so hard to understand.

If the mother doesn't *want* the operation, all the obstetrician has to do is point to the distressed blips on the monitor screen. That's *reality*, what appears on the cathode ray tube, not what the woman feels and wants.

A woman has plenty of other reasons not to want her delivery electronically monitored. In order to attach the electrodes to the fetus' scalp, the bag of waters must be artificially broken. This results in an instant depression of the fetal heart rate. In one study, children whose birth was electronically monitored were sixty-five percent more likely to suffer behavioral or developmental problems later in life.

Of course, what the woman feels and wants is secondary to what the obstetrician says must be. And that includes scheduling the delivery according to the doctor's convenience. In many hospitals the induced, "nine-to-five" delivery has become the rule. Working only from his calculations of when the baby is due—which can be off by as much as six weeks!—the doctor induces labor when he feels like it, not when the baby is naturally ready to pass through the birth canal. A labor induced by the doctor can end up a Caesarean delivery because a baby that's not ready to be born will naturally show more distress on fetal monitors, distress at being summoned prematurely.

Fetal lung disease, failure of normal growth and development, and other mental and physical disabilities associated with premature birth are dangers of induced delivery. As many as four percent of the babies admitted to newborn-intensive care nurseries come in after medically induced deliveries. Mothers, too, are more likely to end up in the intensive care ward after an induced delivery. Postoperative complications occur in half of all women who deliver by Caesarean section. And the maternal death rate is *26 times* higher than in women who deliver vaginally. I propose that we drop the term fetal monitoring and start calling it *fatal* monitoring!

Full-term, regular size babies delivered by Caesarean section are also in danger of a serious lung condition known as hyaline membrane disease or respiratory distress syndrome. This poorly understood, sometimes fatal, and usually unresponsive to treatment condition was once found almost exclusively in premature infants. If a baby delivers normally, the compressing action of the uterus squeezes the chest and lungs as the baby emerges. The fluids and secretions that accumulate in the lungs are then propelled through the bronchial tubes and expelled through the mouth. This does not take place in Caesarean babies.

One study concluded that the incidence of this disease could be reduced at least fifteen percent if obstetricians were more careful about Caesarean deliveries. The same report stated that at least 6,000 of the estimated 40,000 cases of hyaline membrane disease could be prevented if doctors didn't induce delivery until the fetus was mature enough to leave the womb.

Yet the rates of induced deliveries and Caesarean sections are going up, not down. I can remember when if a hospital's incidence of Caesarean deliveries went above four or five percent, there was a full scale investigation. The present level is around twenty-five percent. There are no investigations at all. And in some hospitals the rate is pushing fifty percent.

We tend to get the idea that medicine is always progressing and that surgical procedures are developed, proved useful, and incorporated into everyday practice—at least until they are supplanted by the next "miracle." But that's not the way it happens at all. Surgery goes through three phases, but none of them has the least to do with progress. The first phase a new surgical procedure goes through is enthusiastic acceptance. Of course, the natural order of things says that a new development should be treated with skepticism before enthusiasm. But that's not the way things work in Modern Medicine. Once an operation is proved *possible,* its enthusiastic acceptance is guaranteed. Only after an operation has been around for some time and the real usefulness and *ab*usefulness have had plenty of chances to emerge from the fog of early enthusiasm, does skepticism begin to seep in from around the edges.

Coronary bypass surgery enjoyed unbounded acceptance for the first five or six years. Everyone acted like the operation, in which a blood vessel clogged by fat deposits is surgically "bypassed," was the answer to the catastrophic rate of death by heart attack in the United States. But the lily hasn't been able to stand up to the gilding process. Though tens of thousands of men and women still line up for this operation every year, more and more people are getting skeptical. Apparently, the operation doesn't work as well as surgeons would like to think. A seven-year study by the Veterans Administration of more than 1,000 people found that except for high-risk patients with rare left-main artery disease, the coronary bypass provided no benefit. Mortality rates for surgery patients were not significantly different from those medically treated. In fact, among the low-risk patients, the mortality rates after four years were slightly *higher* among those receiving the operation. Other studies have shown that people who have coronary bypass surgery still show abnormalities on exercise EKG tests and that they have no less risk of suffering a heart attack than those who are treated nonsurgically. Though the operation seems to provide relief from angina pain, some doctors believe this may be either a placebo effect or the result of surgical destruction of nerve pathways. Furthermore, the bypass itself can become clogged and leave the patient right back where he or she started before the operation.

The most effective treatment for heart disease appears to be a radical change in diet from the typical high fat to one in which fat makes up ten percent or less of total calories, combined with a progressive exercise regimen. This treatment has demonstrated evidence of *healing* as well as relief from symptoms.

All of which will eventually push the coronary bypass into the third phase: abandonment.

But operations die hard, especially enormously profitable ones like the bypass. Although it's fairly obvious that replacing a two- or three-inch section of a clogged large vessel isn't going to do anything for the 99.9 percent of clogged arteries that are *left,* the bypass operation still packs 'em in. Fortunes, careers, and lives still depend on it.

Perhaps what it will take to put the bypass under for good is the kind of courage it took one surgeon to pound the last nail into the coffin of "poudrage," a heart operation that was popular a few decades ago. In this operation, they would open up the chest and simply sprinkle talcum powder on the outside of the heart. Presumably, this would irritate the linings and the vessels so they would develop new blood vessels and increase circulation. Poudrage was all the rage until a surgeon took a series of patients for the operation, opened all their chests, but sprinkled the powder on only half of them. The results were exactly the same. They all felt the same after surgery!

Once a surgical procedure is abandoned by all rational pretense, it isn't necessarily abandoned by Modern Medicine. If you take the major categories of surgery, most reached this point years ago. Their real usefulness is hard to find, but they overflow with *sacramental* benefits. As rituals of the Church, they never die. Although tonsillectomies should have been for all *practical* purposes abandoned for 2,000 years, they're still quite popular as a medical ceremony. Ophthalmologists scare the hell out of parents by telling them their child will develop blindness in one eye if his or her mild crossed eye syndrome isn't surgically corrected. If that were true, we would have millions of people walking around blind in one eye, since that's how many cases never reach the ophthalmologists.

And though the bloom is off the rose as far as the coronary bypass is concerned, doctors in Modern Medicine's sacrament mill are developing the same basic—and useless—technique for use on *other* forms of cardiovascular disease!

Modern cancer surgery someday will be regarded with the same kind of horror that we now regard the use of leeches in George Washington's time. It was shown to be irrational thirty-five years ago when Warren Cole at the University of Illinois showed that if you examine the peripheral blood after you open the skin, you find that as a result of surgery the tumor cells have already spread. Doctors answered that by saying of course the tumor spreads, but the rest of the body can take care of it. That's a silly answer. If the person's body could "take care of it," the person wouldn't have cancer in the first place! Some say that cancer surgery is threatened because of all the new techniques for fighting cancer. It's the other way around: the new techniques are capturing people's imagination and hope because cancer surgery is proving a disappointment. Your surgeon, nonetheless, will be the last to admit this.

People ask me why there's so much unnecessary surgery, and I tell them there are more reasons why there *should* be than there are that there *shouldn't* be. The only reason why there shouldn't be so much unnecessary surgery is that it causes suffering and loss of life, health, and expenses that do not have to be. That consideration alone has never had much effect on the workings of the Church of Modern Medicine. On the other hand, the reasons why there *should* be unnecessary surgery are legion, and quite compelling within the ethical framework of the Church.

The simplest reason is that surgery can be put to many uses besides the stated purpose of correcting or removing a disease process. Surgery is a great teaching tool as well as a fertile experimental field—although the only thing that's ever "learned" or "discovered" is how to perform the surgery. When I was Senior Pediatric Consultant to the Department of Mental Health in Illinois, I cut out a certain kind of operation that was being performed on mongoloid children with heart defects. The stated purpose of the operation was to improve oxygen supply to the brain. The real purpose, of course, was to improve the state's residency programs in cardiovascular surgery, because nothing beneficial happened to the brains of mongoloid children—and the surgeons knew that. The whole idea was absurd. And deadly, since the operation had a fairly high mortality rate. Naturally, the university people were very upset when I cut out the operation. They couldn't figure out a better use for the mongoloid children, and, besides, it was important to train people.

Greed plays a role in causing unnecessary surgery, although I don't think the economic motive alone is enough to explain it. There's no doubt that if you eliminated all unnecessary surgery, most surgeons would go out of business. They'd have to look for honest work, because the surgeon gets paid when he performs surgery on you, not when you're treated some other way. In prepaid group practices where surgeons are paid a steady salary not tied to how many operations they perform, hysterectomies and tonsillectomies occur only about one-third as often as in fee-for-service situations.

If we had about one-tenth as many surgeons as we have now, there would be very little unnecessary surgery. Even the American College of Surgeons has said we need only 50,000 to 60,000 board certified surgeons, plus about 10,000 interns and residents, to provide amply for the country's surgical needs for the next half century. According to their projections—which we would expect to be considerate of the financial plight of surgeons if their suggestions were taken seriously—almost *half* of the 100,000 or so surgeons we actually *do* have right now are superfluous. Those 50,000 or so extra unsheathed scalpels do a lot of damage.

Ignorance plays a part in a lot of unnecessary surgery, too. I don't mean ignorance on the part of the patients. If, for example, you eliminated all gynecological surgery that resulted from improper, outdated, and outright stupid obstetrical-gynecological *practice*, there wouldn't be much gynecological surgery left. Doctors know full well, for instance, that women who experience menstrual irregularities are more prone to develop vaginal or cervical cancer if they take oral contraceptives. In fact, the risk for some of these women, depending on what caused their menstrual irregularities, is more than ten times the already increased risk! Yet few doctors bother to find out who these women are before they put them on the Pill. I know of one woman who was taking the Pill for years—unadvised of the danger she was in. She had severe bleeding during her first period, an incident that marked her as someone who should *not* take the Pill. Even when her checkup revealed—via a Pap smear—that something irregular was going on, her gynecologist told her not to worry since she could always get a hysterectomy. Apparently, his motives were a mixture of greed and ignorance, because the next doctor she went to told her that if she didn't have a relatively minor surgical procedure right away, she would definitely need a hysterectomy within a few years. But even *that* minor operation could have been avoided had her doctor informed her of the danger she was in the moment she started taking the Pill.

Greed and ignorance aren't the most important reasons why there is so much unnecessary surgery, however. It's basically a problem of belief: doctors believe in surgery. There's a certain fascination in "going under the knife," and doctors take every advantage of it to get people there. After all, surgery is an element of Progress, and Progress separates us from those who came before us and from those we are *surpassing.* In America, what *can* be done *will* be done. Whether something *should* be done is beside the point. As long as we can build the tools and do it, it *must* be the right thing to do. So not only do we have coronary bypasses, tonsillectomies, and radical mastectomies—but transsexual surgery as well.

The first surgery was religious, and ninety percent of the surgery performed today is also religious. The Jewish ritual circumcision, or *bris,* has a place in Jewish law and culture. The *bris* is performed on the eighth day of life by a trained *mohel* who uses the same technique that has withstood more than 4,000 years of use. Ten men stand by to make sure he does it right, too. Modern Medicine's routine circumcision, however, takes place on the first or second day of life, when blood loss can be especially dangerous. It's performed by a surgeon, or an intern, or a medical student using the "latest" technique. Where the *bris* ceremony includes pouring some wine in the infant's mouth, no anesthetic at all is used in Modern Medicine's ritual.

Routine circumcision of all males makes no sense outside of a religious framework. A circumcision is an operation, and its dangers are not inconsiderable. It's not altogether rare for a surgeon to get smart and use cautery instead of a knife—and to slip and burn off most of the penis.

In some primitive religions submitting to ritual mutilation elevates the victim to a higher consciousness. Through either the intense pain of the mutilation or the effects of drugs—or both—the victim hallucinates communion with the deities. Sometimes this "privilege" is reserved for the priesthood or for certain communicants of special status. In Christianity, only Jesus and the martyrs were graced with mutilation—except for a dubious mystic every now and then who miraculously bears the "stigmata," or the wounds of Christ.

In the Church of Modern Medicine, *no one* is excluded from the sacrifice. Until the invention of anesthesia, victims gritted their teeth and saw their gods with the clarity agony brings—until they passed out. Now the victim is "put under" in a form of mock death, so the surgeon not only has the opportunity to heal him, but bring him back from the dead as well. Of course, even that opportunity has been superceded by the refinement of local anesthesia. Now the victim can stay awake and observe the surgeon fiddling with his mortality. After the operation, of course, even children enjoy showing off their scars. If they're the children of doctors, chances are better that they'll have scars to show off, because doctors' families tend to have more surgery than anybody else. Which demonstrates that doctors believe in the sacrament's power at least as faithfully as they expect everybody else to.

One of the true tests of a fanatic is whether or not he takes his own medicine—or believes his own press releases. The fact that doctors do get in line for the sacrifice only strengthens its grounding in ceremony.

The most sinister aspect of Modern Medicine's belief in surgery is the presumption that lies behind that belief, that the priest can overcome anything because he can operate on you. *You don't have to take care of yourself, we can fix you if you go wrong.* All you have to do is believe enough to show up for the sacrament, which in this case is a ritual mutilation. Modern Medicine has succeeded in usurping the power of traditional religions so all of us, including the priests, rabbis, ministers, and monks, see ourselves as ultimately repairable *to* and *by* the power that resides in the tabernacle of the operating room.

To protect yourself from your doctor's belief in surgery and avoid the knife's sacramental use on your own flesh, your first step is to educate yourself. Once again, make it your business to learn more about your case than your doctor does. Books, journals, and magazines available at the public library should provide you with enough information.

You should be especially wary if your doctor recommends one of the common operations, such as tonsillectomy, hysterectomy, umbilical hernia repair, etc. Remember that the doctor doesn't view surgery as a potentially harmful invasion of your body, but as a beneficent ceremony that can't help but bestow some good. Even a trusted family doctor cannot be trusted to prescribe surgery *only* when it's really necessary.

You should start asking questions the moment the doctor mentions surgery. What is this operation supposed to accomplish? How does it do it? What will happen if I don't have surgery? Are there any alternatives to surgery? What are the chances the operation will not succeed in what it's supposed to do? After you've obtained your doctor's answers, you should check out everything he says on your own. Chances are good that you will find conflicting information if you dig deep enough. That's the idea.

Get a second opinion. Don't go to a doctor in the same group practice, or even to one on the same hospital staff. You may have to go out of town to reach a really independent doctor. You should ask the second doctor the very same questions that you asked the first. If you get two widely different opinions, you should first go back to the original doctor and confront him with the information. That still may not resolve the differences to your satisfaction. In that case, ask your general practitioner to hold an old fashioned consultation at which all the doctors are present with you.

This may sound like a lot of trouble to go to. But you should keep in mind that the ultimate goal is to keep you in one piece unless absolutely necessary. Don't be afraid to get a third or even a fourth opinion. Considering the enormous quantity of unnecessary surgery, the chances are quite good that what your doctor's recommending is also unnecessary. You should always keep this in mind, especially when the doctor tries to make you feel like surgery is the only answer to your problem. Not only might it not be the only answer, but it might be no answer at all. You might not even have a problem!

Don't hesitate to confront your doctor with whatever information, opinions, and feelings you gather from your "homework." You're bound to learn something from his reaction. Don't be afraid to rely on the opinions of friends, neighbors, family members, and people whom you believe have wisdom.

If you decide that surgery isn't the answer, do whatever you have to do to detach yourself from the situation. Don't be afraid of offending the doctor. Although it's best to simply declare the fact that you don't want the operation and you're not going to have it, you may feel better playing the "I'll think about it" game. Once your doctor has tried to persuade you to have surgery, he may not be able to retreat from that position and continue as your doctor. After all, if he has told you that surgery is the only avenue, he can't very well treat you some other way can he? One way or the other, if your decision to stay in one piece means you lose a doctor, you're better off.

If, on the other hand, you decide to have the operation, you still shouldn't lie back and let the ceremony proceed quite yet. Contrary to what most doctors would have you believe, it does make a lot of difference *who* performs the surgery. Why shouldn't it? It makes a difference who paints your house or fixes your car doesn't it? Isn't it reasonable that talent should also make a difference in who removes your gall bladder?

People often ask me how to go about picking a surgeon if they "must" have surgery. I always say that if you really "must" have surgery, you're most likely in no position to make a choice because the only "must have" situation I recognize is the emergency. And in an emergency you don't have a choice. If you're in an accident and you need surgery, you take any surgeon you can get. In any situation short of an emergency, you've got plenty of time not only to decide whether or not you need the surgery but also who should perform the operation.

Again, you start to pick a surgeon by asking questions. You should talk to several surgeons and ask each and every one: How many times have you done this operation? What's your batting average? How many of the operations have been successful? How many haven't? What's your rate of complications? What is the death rate from this operation? How many of your patients have died during or shortly after this operation? Can you refer me to some of your patients who've had this operation? Would they be willing to talk to me?

My favorite question to ask a surgeon is, "If you were out of town when the operation was performed, who would you recommend for the operation?" A variation of that is, "If *you* needed the operation, doctor, who would you go to?"

You should also be asking the surgeons *what kind* of surgery is necessary. You might be able to get away with less radical surgery than originally recommended. And don't neglect to ask each surgeon, once again, if the operation is necessary. This may sound like a waste of time once you've already decided to have the operation. But you may come across new information, or a doctor who does have an alternative treatment. In any case, if you are exposed to new information, hit the books again and check it out.

If the surgical procedure is extremely complex, it might be a good idea to call whatever surgeon has a reputation for the operation. If he is in another city and you don't want to travel—or he doesn't want to take on another case—ask him to refer you to someone closer or someone who will take you on. You should also ask friends and family members to help out in finding the right surgeon. I also have a healthy respect for the ability of the average clergyman to pick out a good doctor. No matter who refers you, or what the reputation of the surgeon, you should *never* let down your guard and let things go by that you don't understand to your satisfaction.

And that goes double *after* the operation. If the operation doesn't work out as planned, or if you suffer side effects that don't seem called for, waste no time in having them checked out. As with the side effects of a drug, the discomfort may be temporary and harmless. Or it may be deadly. When you approach a different doctor with post-operative problems, you should challenge him with the following questions: Can you give me an honest opinion with regard to the other doctor's performance on this operation? Would you give me an honest opinion even though it were to result in a malpractice suit against the other doctor? Or against your hospital?

Depending on how he answers these questions, you can decide whether or not to trust him. In this and any other medical situation, your reluctance to give away your trust is your first defense. Make every doctor earn it, especially if he wants to mutilate you.

4
The Temples of Doom

A hospital is like a war. You should try your best to stay out of it. And if you get into it you should take along as many allies as possible and get out as soon as you can.

For the amount of money the average hospital stay costs, you could spend an equal length of time at just about *any* resort in the world, transportation included. And unless your condition required emergency treatment, your health might be better off if you spent the time and money at the resort, too. For the hospital is the Temple of the Church of Modern Medicine, and thus one of the most dangerous places on earth.

When a culture develops to the point where its citizens live in houses, the gods of the people have to reside somewhere, too. A temple is built to house the spirit of the religion. Whatever vision informs the religion is present in the temple, and the building becomes the center of prophecy, the place where the gods speak to the people. When I hear someone—usually an older person who wasn't born in this country—say that the hospital is "where you go to die," I say to myself that he or she has been hearing what the gods are saying.

Children, again, provide us with a message from their unclouded perception: kids are unabashedly afraid of going to the hospital. Just as their fear of doctors is something we could all cultivate to our advantage, so is their fear of hospitals. Of course, a child would be hard pressed to articulate his or her fear. Even most adults would have a hard time isolating and describing exactly what specific things he or she is afraid of in the hospital. Besides, adults are *afraid* to admit fear. Priests of the Temple take advantage of ignorance and reticence by assuring us, "There's nothing to be afraid of."

There's plenty to be afraid of. The God that resides in the Temple of Modern Medicine is Death.

There are germs in hospitals that you can't get anywhere else in town, not only because hospitals are such dirty places, but because of Modern Medicine's fetish for ritual purification. Now, that appears to be a contradictory statement, but it's not. Hospitals aren't kept anywhere near as clean as they should be. Housekeeping staffs are generally smaller than necessary. Whenever you have an overworked staff, the tendency is for only the *obvious* jobs to get done, and not that carefully, either. So what you're liable to find if you look closely is dust and dirt in corners and other out of the way places. *Hospital* dust and dirt isn't the kind of dust and dirt you find anywhere.

Where else can you find all in one building: animal and vegetable waste from food preparation, rubbish and trash, biological wastes from diagnostic, medical, surgical, autopsy, and wound dressing activities, bandages, discarded tissues from surgery and autopsy, sputum, placentas, organs, amputated limbs, sacrificed research animals, disposable diapers and underpads, catheters, soap, bodily secretions, cups, masks, swabs, sanitary napkins, plaster casts, syringes, and fecal material? All of this goes down the same chute, collected and thrown by the same people—people who have access to patients' bedrooms and operating rooms as well as the kitchen, laboratories, and morgue.

In one hospital, it was discovered that stretchers used to transport patients also were used to carry cadavers. That's bad enough, but these stretchers still bore the residue from their prior grim journeys. In this same hospital, which by the way is a large public hospital in Washington, D.C., "organic residue and fecal material" were also found in emergency rooms, floors, and working areas in the morgue. In patients' rooms, soiled dressings, dirty shower stalls, hypodermic needles, and heavy accumulations of dust were found.

Such discoveries don't shock me anymore, since I've realized that these conditions are the rule rather than the exception. And what makes these situations even more dangerous are the hospital heating and air conditioning systems which blow the dust and germs all over the hospital. Not to mention the plumbing system. Hospitals have more plumbing than any ordinary building. Besides the usual hot and cold water, hospitals have chilled water, distilled water, vacuum systems, fluid suction systems, oxygen, sprinkling systems for fire (most of which are inadequate), refrigerant, recirculated cooling water, drainage systems, sewage systems, and irrigation systems—all going through their walls and floors. Not only are the chances for accidental cross connection enormous, but so are the chances that illegal connections will increase the dangers of cross-contamination.

Modern Medicine's fanatical devotion to purification ironically multiplies the dangers of creating a class of germs which are resistant to antibiotics. In chapter two I talked about how the overuse of antibiotics gives rise to bacteria which are resistant to the drugs. What better breeding ground for these supergerms could there be than a modern hospital, where antibiotics flow like soup? Some bacteria even adapt to the point where they *feed* on the antibiotics!

Then what happens, of course, is that the hospital staff becomes a walking culture dish for these germs. Since they're exposed to them everyday, however, they aren't harmed by them. But that doesn't do *you* any good when the housekeeper or the nurse handles your bedding, your food, your clothes, and you.

The priests of the Temple, the doctors, are even worse spreaders of disease. Doctors neglect to wash their hands, unless it's before the sacrament of surgery, where it's part of the ritual. Usually they casually go from sick patient to sick patient, handling tongue depressors, syringes, and various parts of the patients. Yet they seem to feel that there's something uniquely clean about themselves, and they don't wash their hands in between. Doctors also have great confidence in caps, masks, and rubber gloves—none of which deserves any confidence at all. Masks become so contaminated after just ten minutes that they serve as bacterial *cultures* rather than shields. Rubber gloves often are contaminated, too.

When I walk into a newborn nursery wearing a clean suit that I just put on that morning, the nurses always make a fuss and make me put on a robe. I make fun of it by asking them if they're insulting my new suit. Their behavior shows that they have placed their trust in the *sacred vestments* rather than their own perception of reality. There's no guarantee that the white robe they make me put on is any cleaner than my suit. In fact, there's evidence to the contrary. That white robe may have been sitting on the shelf for months. How do they know it was properly laundered? Especially since it was no doubt thrown into the same tub as soiled sheets, pillow cases, and operating room linens. Just because it's white doesn't mean it's clean. The same goes for the bedding. The linens may be washed, but the mattresses and pillows are not.

Overall, your chances of getting an infection in the hospital are about one in twenty. That's a conservative estimate. Half of the infections in hospitals are caused by contaminated medical devices such as catheters and intravenous equipment. Before the explosion in the use of these devices around 1965, device-related infections were virtually nonexistent. About 15,000 people die from hospital-acquired infections every year. As in the case of drug deaths, hospital staff will fudge statistics when a seriously ill patient succumbs to a hospital-acquired infection. Your chances also depend on what you're in the hospital for. If you go for an operation, you're not only going to be exposed to the operating room dangers, but your body will be seriously weakened by the surgery and won't be able to fight off infections as well. If you've been burned or wounded, you'll also be weakened and therefore more likely to get an infection.

In my experience, a one in twenty risk would have to be the *base line* risk representing the minimum danger of infection. I've seen epidemics spread through hospitals so fast that everybody had to be sent home. Pediatric wards and newborn nurseries are the most vulnerable to spreading infections. It's a well-kept secret in hospitals that the most dangerous place in the hospital—as far as the patients are concerned—is the newborn nursery, where none of the patients have (particularly those who are denied the immunity-transference of breastfeeding) developed their immunity to germs.

As bacteriologically overrun as hospitals are, I've rarely seen an epidemic that was blamed on the hospital or the staff. They always pin it on the *visitors!* The inevitable aftermath of the epidemic is restriction of visiting hours. Actually, keeping visitors away is only *half* of what should be done. *Patients* would be better off if they were kept out of the hospitals, too.

Hospitals are contaminated with more than germs. Remember, since hospitals are the temples of Modern Medicine, all the dangerous *chemicals* that doctors love to use are in plentiful supply. With all those drugs at their disposal, doctors are bound to use them. And they do. Patients in the hospital receive an average of twelve different drugs. But even if you're not drugged to death or disability, there are other chemicals floating around that can make your stay less than healthy. In the first place, your doctor may not be using drugs, but everyone else's doctor *is*. Poisonous solvents used in laboratories and cleaning facilities, flammable chemicals, and radioactive wastes all threaten you with contamination.

If hospitals were the sharply efficient places they pretend to be, we could rest less uneasily about these dangers. Unfortunately, hospitals are virtual *models* of ineptitude. There are so many *simple* mistakes—mistakes in which someone has two or three choices and chooses *wrong*—that you must feel extremely apprehensive when you start to contemplate all the opportunities for *complex* errors!

Everything gets mixed up in hospitals—including patients. My brother went to the hospital for a hernia operation many years ago. He was scheduled for surgery at 11 a.m. I went up to his room at 9:30, but he wasn't there. I knew right away what had happened. I ran down to the operating room, and sure enough, there he was. They'd taken him instead of another patient. The only reason he escaped was that the other patient was supposed to get a hysterectomy.

Mixups occur in hospitals all the time. Surgeons operate on the wrong leg. Medicines are given to the wrong patients. The wrong food is served to people on special diets. Even babies are mixed up. Hardly a year goes by without some story appearing in the newspapers about a colossal mixup of babies and mothers at a local hospital. No doctor who has had any experience in maternity wards has not seen the wrong baby brought to the mother by the nurse and the nurse corrected by the mother. There are twenty to thirty babies in the average nursery. Every doctor knows footprints are not reliable, and those arm bands are always falling off. So who knows one from the other?

Not only are people mixed up in hospitals, they're *lost,* too. Newspaper stories have told of patients found dead in hospital elevators and little-used bathrooms. Two years ago a baby was stolen from the University of Chicago Hospital. Every time I go by the newborn nursery at Michael Reese Hospital, I stir up the nurses by asking if anyone there has heard from the Fronzack baby. More than a decade ago, the Fronzack baby simply *disappeared* from their nursery and was never found. About a year ago, there was a case in Israel in which two mothers were given the wrong babies. It wasn't found out until the babies were two months old. At first, neither mother would exchange "her" baby. What do you call someone who's been your mother for two months?

As far as I'm concerned, one of the best arguments for having your baby at home is the distinct possibility that you'll go home from the hospital with the wrong baby.

Another hazard that threatens you in the hospital is the likelihood of an accident. In a suburban hospital in Pennsylvania, it was discovered that oxygen and nitrous oxide labels were accidentally switched when a construction crew installed gas lines in the emergency room. Until the mixup was discovered, people who should have been getting nitrous oxide were getting oxygen and people who were supposed to get oxygen were getting nitrous oxide. It took six months for the hospital to discover the error. The hospital admitted to five deaths from the accident, but said that all *thirty-five* deaths in the emergency room during that period were not caused by the switch because some of those were dead on arrival and some were too far gone to benefit from oxygen even if they had received it. If that sounds like the kind of fudging doctors use to cover up a treatment-related death, you're getting my message.

As doctors rely more and more on technology, hospitals become more and more littered with electronic gear and wiring, and the chances of being electrocuted rise right along with the electric bill. In the same Washington, D.C., hospital cited earlier for filth, three patients and several doctors and nurses were severely shocked and burned by faulty electrical equipment in the coronary care unit. This type of accident is not uncommon, and it will grow more common as hospital maintenance staffs shrink and become less able to cope with complex wiring.

So loosely organized and run are most hospitals that *murder* is even a clear and present danger. Witness the deliberate injection of paralyzing drugs to patients at a Michigan Veterans Administration hospital. Deadly drugs are so widely available and so loosely controlled that the hospital couldn't even begin to look for the culprit. The FBI had to be called in. If you want to commit the perfect crime, do it in a hospital.

Of course, you could make a case that hospitals are *already* getting away with murder. If the drugs, the germs, the surgery, the chemicals, or the accidents don't get you, you still stand a good chance of *starving* to death. One of the first major studies of the scandalous state of hospital nutrition examined every surgery patient in a large Boston municipal hospital. They were tested for protein-calorie malnutrition, a *minimal* standard which tells only whether the person is getting enough protein and calories every day over a period of time. Whether the patients were getting enough vitamins and minerals was not tested. Nonetheless, *half* of the surgery patients were *not* getting enough protein and calories. Half of these were severely malnourished: they were malnourished enough to threaten their recovery and lengthen their stay in the hospital. Since they weren't given enough *food* by the hospital, you can be sure they weren't getting enough vitamins or minerals.

The results of this study are by no means uncommon. Many studies since have discovered malnutrition in anywhere from twenty-five to fifty percent of patients in American and British hospitals. The doctor who carried out the Boston study, George L. Blackburn, has since stated that malnutrition is one of the most common causes of death among old people in hospitals. That's not really such a startling statement, in light of facts Dr. Blackburn uncovered. Malnutrition obviously puts a person in the worst possible state to fight off whatever disease brought him to the hospital in the first place. Add to that the dangers and stresses of the hospital, and you have a recipe for disaster. Of course, we can only guess about the true magnitude of that disaster. As with drugs, accidents, and other treatment-related deaths, doctors fudge. We don't know exactly how many people die directly or indirectly from malnutrition in hospitals. What we do know, however, is that a lot of people are malnourished in hospitals, that malnourishment is deadly, and that a lot of people die in hospitals.

Why are people malnourished in hospitals? As bad as most hospital food is, if it were eaten it most likely would prevent most of the protein-calorie malnutrition these studies turn up. The problem is that it's *not* eaten. Nobody sees to it that the patient eats. At best, the tray is brought in and set beside the bed on a table. And there it sits. At worst, the hospital schedule and staff gang up on the patient to keep him or her from touching the food: time for lab tests, time for therapy, time for an enema, time for drugs, time for this and time for that.

Plenty goes on in the Temple of Modern Medicine simply to make you lose your appetite. The psychological dangers of the hospital are every bit as deadly as the physical dangers.

Your hospital stay from the moment you walk in the front door until the moment you walk—or are carried—out has a psychological effect on you similar to a hex or a voodoo curse. Whether you consciously acknowledge it or not, hospital procedures and environment encourage despair and debilitation rather than hope and support. Nobody's optimistic. You see the long faces of the people suffering and dying, and you see the faces of the people who must watch them suffer and die. You see the hospital staff denature their responses and become machines. And then *you* are denatured at the admissions desk as you are reduced to a collection of numbers and symptoms belonging not to you but to the *doctor*. You leave your former world and identity behind. You're literally stripped of your former life as you take off your clothes and hide them and your personal belongings in a closet—artifacts of your real life. That past life is kept from reasserting its ties with you—your relatives are restricted from spending more than token amounts of time with you.

The effect of all these psychological pins is that you relinquish any notion you may have had about having control over your health. Your captors isolate you, alienate you, scare you, depress you, and generally make you feel so anxious that you submit to their every wish. Your spirit broken, you are ready to be a Good Patient.

Children and older people seem to be especially susceptible to the damaging effects of hospital voodoo. Children react very rapidly with strong feelings of abandonment and separation anxiety. Add to this the fear the child has of the operation or whatever they're going to do to him or her. It's no mystery why children who have had as little as one or two nights in the hospital without their parents regress in their behavior to where they lose their toilet training or their ability to speak. Every doctor should know that the ages between three and six are years of great confusion. Kids hardly know what's going on at that age. To subject them to the hospital environment without the benefit of a parent close by is patent cruelty.

More than twenty years ago, I wrote a paper about children's fantasies before a hernia operation. I interviewed kids and asked them what they thought was going to happen to them. Almost every child thought something was going to happen to his genitals. When I asked them where on their body the operation was going to take place, some of them actually *grabbed* their genitals defensively. That was an eye-opener for me. Our conclusion at the time was that children should be counseled before surgery and have the operation explained to them. Now, I know that doesn't do any good. What they really need is to be assured that their parents will be with them throughout the hospitalization. That's what we *should have* advised.

I still don't like to make rounds through hospitals at night: too many crying babies. I always have a lot of trouble with crying babies—I can't ignore them. When I used to make night rounds regularly I would pick up the crying babies or the little kids and carry them out to the nurses' station. If they could sit on the nurses' laps or on the edge of the desk they wouldn't cry.

Adults and the elderly also suffer from a hospital stay. Dr. David Green has called hospitals "the worst place in the world for aged people." I don't disagree with him, except that I would say that hospitals are the worst place in the world for *everybody*. I don't know how we can expect children not to be harmed by the super stresses of a hospital stay when those stresses are so hard on adults. Ironically, we expect the kids to act like super adults in the hospital and adjust to the separation and the fear—while we expect the adults to adjust to being treated like helpless children. Hospital procedures have absolutely no respect for a person's dignity. You have to take off your own clothes and wear a hospital gown that leaves you immodestly vulnerable to inspection and attack by innumerable doctors, nurses, and technicians. You have to lie down most of the time. You can't come and go as you please. And you have to eat what they serve you—if there's time. Then, to top it off, you have to sleep in a room with strangers—*sick* strangers at that!

Hospitalization degrades you. In my twenty-five years of practicing and witnessing the practice of medicine, I've never seen a degrading experience that did anybody's health any good. But remember, hospitals are the temples of Modern Medicine. When you enter the temple of another religion, you enter the presence of that religion's deities. No gods will allow you to take rival gods into their house, so you leave behind your old gods and all that they taught you before you enter. Since the Church views *all* aspects of life that contribute to health as rival gods, you must leave your identity, your family, your confidence, and your dignity at the temple door. Only when you've been purified of your real life can you be eligible for the sinister rewards of the Church of Death's sacraments.

I'm always fascinated when one kind of epidemic or another spreads through a hospital so fast that everybody has to be sent home or transferred to another hospital. Usually, very few people have to be transferred to other hospitals. We always manage to send nine out of ten patients *home* with no problems.

About twenty-five years ago, I decided to conduct a little experiment to find out just how necessary hospitalization really is. I was in charge of a hospital ward that had about twenty-eight beds. I decided that none of the twenty-four patients already there would stay unless they absolutely required hospitalization. I also had control of admissions. So when someone came to be admitted, we decided whether or not they really had to be. We had special procedures available to allow people to be treated at home. We could, for example, pay their taxi fare for outpatient visits, and we had a truck we could use to go out to adjust patients' devices if they were in traction.

I kept this up until we got down to three or four patients. I figured I had pretty well proved that hospitals weren't necessary. I found out afterwards that *I* was the one who wasn't necessary. The nursing office started to complain because the nurses in my ward had nothing to do and were in danger of being transferred. The interns and residents complained that they did not have enough teaching material. That was the end of my experiment on hospital utilization.

Hospitals exist in such aggressive abundance for the convenience of the medical profession, not for the good of the people they're supposed to serve. Hospitals started out as "poor houses" where doctors could send patients who didn't have the money to pay for their services. After awhile, doctors realized that it was much easier for them to have *all* their patients in one place, with all the machinery right there. Naturally, as medicine becomes less personal and more mechanical, it becomes increasingly convenient for the doctor to manage patients in the hospital. It's a well-known fact that a doctor has to be *sharper* and more skillful if he treats people on an outpatient basis. As talent and consideration have become rare commodities among doctors, hospitals have burgeoned. Insurance companies drive people into hospitals by refusing to pay for outpatient treatments. If we didn't recognize that hospital and medical insurance payments were really indulgences to keep a corrupt Church solvent, we would bridle at the absurdity of an insurance company preferring to pay thousands of dollars for treatment in the hospital that could be performed out of hospital for hundreds.

Modern Medicine doesn't have to account for absurdities—or for the dangers of hospitals. Hospitals are, for practical purposes, self-accredited. The boards and committees that decide whether or not a hospital should be allowed to carry on are made up of the same "good ol' boys" that run the hospital. Even when a federal agency enters the picture, the massive institutional inertia of the system keeps bad hospitals operating and discourages adequate reform of bad practices in all hospitals. A few years ago, the Department of Health, Education, and Welfare (HEW) spot-checked 105 hospitals for dangers that were specifically mentioned in the Medicare law. They found sixty-nine hospitals failed to meet the specifications regarding fire safety, drug records, size of nursing staff, number of doctors, dietary supervision, medical records, and medical libraries. All of the hospitals had *recently* been passed by the Joint Commission on Accreditation of Hospitals, and after the HEW test results were made known, the JCAH refused to withdraw accreditation of the offending hospitals.

Public outcry over hospital conditions have spawned what I call a "haunted house full of ghost reforms." Most of these reforms take place either on paper or in secret meetings of the people who run the hospital. The Church is not about to give up any power, especially where its own temple is concerned. Would Catholics allow Jews to tell them how to run their churches and schools? Reforms such as hospital ombudsmen and patient advocates to review and act on patients' complaints are set up merely to run interference on malpractice suits. They lull the patients into thinking that their rights are being looked after. More than two years after the American Hospital Association "formally adopted" the "Patient's Bill of Rights" and distributed it to all member hospitals, only a fraction of the hospitals had made the "rights" available to patients.

We can't really expect the temples of Modern Medicine to enact these reforms, since the very idea that a patient has any rights is totally contrary to the operating concept of the institution. Furthermore, if the patients' rights were really looked after, the hospitals would be *closed!* It's been known for some time that we simply have too many hospitals and that people do not need to spend anywhere near the amount of time in the hospital that is presently routine. Numerous studies have shown over the years that most lengthy hospital stays are unnecessary. Five days, three days, or even half a day in the hospital for childbirth is *at best* unnecessary. Usually, it's downright harmful to both mother and baby. The length of time in the hospital that heart patients can profit from is rapidly diminishing, according to the scientific literature. Whereas doctors once could point to studies that showed that a month was the *minimum,* we're finding out now that a three-week stay is no better than a two-week stay, that a one-week stay might be still better, and that patients treated *at home, on their feet* do even better! Even the American Hospital Association admits that we've got more hospital beds than we need, so you can just imagine how grossly obvious the superfluous hospitals really are to those who can see what's going on.

Of course, the AHA and other Church agencies do their best to keep the public from finding out what *is* going on. The privately funded (with the money you pay the hospitals) Commission on Professional and Hospital Activities maintains a computer bank of information on what goes on in American hospitals, including comparative death rates for procedures, accidents, infections, errors—everything you've got to be afraid of in hospitals. Just try to take a peek at this information. The Commission guards it with a vengeance the government would envy. For good reason. When explaining why the information is "classified," Commission and AHA spokespeople will tell you that the "information could be misinterpreted and could discourage the kind of analysis that leads to improvement." What they mean is that the public would "misinterpret" hospital shortcomings as so dangerous that they wouldn't be caught dead in them. And, of course, that would "discourage improvement" because there wouldn't be anything to improve: the hospitals would close! I suggest that this computer bank contains the potential for a "Pentagon Papers" and "Watergate" combined.

It's well-known that Modern Medicine doesn't act on scientific knowledge until public awareness grows strong enough to *demand* it. Research is the *prayer* of the religion of Modern Medicine. Research is OK as long as you don't *act* on it. A doctor doing research can ruin his career in the eyes of Modern Medicine merely by overstepping that line and *advocating* that his research results be implemented!

Whether the Temple or any of what goes on inside does good or harm is irrelevant. What's important is that the faithful *are* faithful and that they show their belief by showing up for the sacraments, which are sold not on the basis of what they do but what they're supposed to do. All their intentions may be good, but everybody knows what the road to hell is paved with.

Besides, Modern Medicine's *intentions* can be counted on to be corrupt, too. When hospitals started relaxing visiting hours, they didn't do it because they realized that people should be allowed to be with their family. They did it because pediatrics was dying and the beds in the pediatric wards were empty. They would have done anything to get children in there—let mothers, fathers, siblings, cats, or dogs in for a visit! Obstetrics is dying, too. People want to have their babies at home, not in the hospital. So today they'll let *anybody* in the delivery room, husband, sister, mother, boyfriend . . . *anybody*! As long as they get the revenue.

What they're counting on is that people will be lulled into feeling that the hospital really is the place for them, that the Temple really can save them. Of course, it can't. The Temple has nothing to do with health. There are no facilities in hospitals for health or for any of the things commonly recognized as contributing to health. The food is as bad as you'd find in the worst fast food drive-in. There are no facilities for exercise. All the personal factors that can make you well or keep you healthy are removed—family, friends, and sense of *self*. In no uncertain terms, when you walk into a hospital, you are surrendering—"Here I am, totally unable to help myself. You must save me. I am without power. All power is yours."

Hospital costs are the biggest single element in the country's total bill for medical "care." That bill is rapidly overtaking defense, the Number One item on the country's total bill for everything. When medicine *exceeds* defense, the Inquisition will really be unstoppable. No one seriously challenges whatever institution is the first item on the budget. Whatever costs more than anything else gathers bureaucratic inertia of such immense proportions that it controls the destiny of the country. Then the dream of Modern Medicine will be fulfilled: the whole country will become a hospital. We'll all be patients in the Temple of Doom.

The first thing you should do to protect yourself against the dangers of the modern hospital is to resolve to avoid unnecessary hospitalization. Since most people are in the hospital because their doctor put them there, you simply should *not* let your doctor put you there. That means not taking drugs unless absolutely necessary and not having surgery unless absolutely necessary. (See the previous two chapters.)

There are many common procedures that doctors won't do on an outpatient basis—unless you insist. Here is where, once again, you have to do some homework that will put you one up on the doctor as far as knowing what can and can't be done. More than ninety-five percent of births to healthy women, for example, can and should be done outside the hospital. Yet doctors still scare young mothers and fathers into the delivery-operating room with horror stories of "complications" which are, in truth, statistical fantasies or complications which *result* from obstetrical intervention. Now that the scare tactics haven't diminished the home birth movement, we see more and more "birthing rooms" appearing in hospitals.

Don't kid yourself into thinking that birthing rooms made up to look just like a real (motel) bedroom are going to make any difference. Once you allow yourself to be lured onto Modern Medicine's turf, they've got you. I have a recurring dream of a nice young couple going into the birthing room, like the one at Illinois Masonic Hospital—complete with brass bed and color TV set. The doctor smiles and acts just like a friendly uncle. But once the mother is strapped into the brass bed, the doctor pushes a button on a secret panel and the papered walls slide away, the furniture disappears, and they're suddenly in an operating room under the glare of the operating light with the surgeon standing there scalpel in hand ready to slice her belly from one end to the other.

That fantasy isn't so unreal. Birthing rooms are not so isolated from the operating rooms that the brass bed can't be rolled into action before the young mother and father know what's going on. If you're on the doctor's turf, you play by the doctor's rules. Whereas if you have your baby at home, the doctor has to do *his* homework. If you need the hospital facilities, you should use them. But if you can have your baby in a birthing room, you can have it in your own bedroom.

In protecting yourself from your doctor's tendency to send you to the hospital unnecessarily, you should use the same tactics discussed in avoiding drugs and surgery. Educate yourself to the possibilities, alternatives, and consequences. If that means going to other doctors, do it. If it means going to healers that aren't medical doctors, do it. Don't be afraid to confront your doctor with the information you gather. Of course, what you're really doing is searching for the right doctor. And that, actually, is exactly how you should go about finding the right *hospital*—if you decide that you need one. Conventional wisdom preaches that the best hospital is the one which is heavily involved in *teaching,* one that has lots of students, lots of house officers, lots of research. That wisdom may have been valid thirty or forty years ago when there were some pretty peculiar things going on in community hospitals. But it's nonsense today—unless you want to feel like the frogs, crayfish, and fetal pigs in a biology class. If you want to find the hospitals that have the highest rates of nosocomial (doctors' jargon for hospital-acquired) infection, that make the most mistakes regarding lab tests and dispensing drugs, that mix up more patients, and that do more psychological damage—then go to teaching or research hospitals. If you want to be used for someone else's purpose—whether it's to demonstrate the right (wrong?!) way to perform a procedure or to find out if this or that drug really works—you couldn't go to a better place than a teaching hospital.

There used to be another piece of conventional wisdom which stated that if you had a very rare or serious condition you were better off in a teaching hospital. That's no longer true, either. The teaching hospitals are there, don't forget, to teach the *orthodox* treatments. What you're going to get is the orthodox treatment, whether it works or not. If you want to get the latest, unorthodox treatment, you have to go to a smaller hospital or even one outside the reach of the Church—out of the country.

Don't choose a hospital at all, because hospitals don't treat patients, doctors do. Choose a doctor. If you've chosen the right doctor, chances are he will have chosen the right workshop for his skills. Most of the doctors I know who fall into that category of good doctors spend very little of their time in big teaching or research hospitals. The mythical three-legged stool of medicine—research, teaching, and patient care—is not a stool at all because the legs aren't equal. Patient care almost always gets the short leg when doctors and hospitals try to make a stool out of it. So if someone tells me they have chosen a teaching hospital, I tell them to be on their guard because they're in serious danger.

No matter who your doctor is and what hospital he or she has put you in, you're *always* in mortal danger, so you *always* should be on your guard. Not passively, either. Your job is to make trouble. Trouble for the nurses, trouble for the doctors, trouble for everyone. Subvert the system that will steal your dignity and maybe your life if you let it.

That's not always easy to do. If you hold a high rank in society, you can do it fairly easily. When the wife of the chairman of the board goes in, he often gets a suite right next to hers. If you're not very highly placed, you've got to use whatever muscle you have. You've got to be prepared, cunning, and skillful.

I like mothers and fathers to stay with their children while they're in the hospital. In one of the hospitals I worked in, parents could stay with the child only if he or she was on the critical list. So I would put *all* of the kids on the critical list! They left me alone on that for a long time—until the showdown.

The visiting hours were supposed to end at 7:30 every evening.

One mother called me and said her child was crying but that he would stop crying and go to sleep by 8:30 if only she could stay with him until 8:30. I told her to go up to his room and stay. Then the nurse called me and said that this woman has to leave because the child wasn't critical and visiting hours were over. I asked her what she would do if the mother decided to stay. She said she'd call the supervisor. I called the supervisor and asked her the same question. She said she'd call the hospital administrator.

The administrator called me and I asked *him* what he planned to do. He said he'd have a police guard come and escort the woman out of the hospital. I asked him to do me a favor and hold off for fifteen minutes so I could see what I could do. He figured I was a nice guy and would take care of it for him, so he agreed.

I called up a local TV newsman—an activist—and told him I had a mother who was about to be thrown out of the hospital because she wanted to stay with her crying child for an extra hour until he went to sleep. He asked me to hold them off for twenty minutes so he could rush cameras to the scene. I said I'd see what I could do, and I'd get back to him. Then I called up the administrator and asked him to hold off for just twenty minutes more because the TV camera crew was on the way to film the policeman escorting the woman out of the hospital.

The administrator said, "All right, Bob, you win. You call off your dogs, and I'll call off mine. But tomorrow I want to see you in my office." Next morning I went to his office and he told me he could throw me off the staff for doing what I did. I told him I knew that, but that I also knew that he wasn't going to do it. Because if he did I would go right to the newspaper and make the biggest fuss he'd ever seen. He said that was right. And he made a deal with me: "Your patients' visitors can stay as long as they want, but nobody else's. I don't want you to bring this up with the rest of the staff."

That's the way it was. Some of the nurses used to be frightened of me, or just plain mad at me, because I always demanded that my patients receive whatever I thought they should have *ahead* of everybody else. The nurse would say, "But Dr. Mendelsohn, there are twenty-seven other patients on the floor. Why should yours come first?" And I would tell her that my patients *did* come first, because if they didn't I was going to raise the biggest holler in the world. My patients did get taken care of first most of the time. I used to violate the rules all the time.

Which is exactly what you have to do to protect yourself when you are in the hospital. You can't do it alone. You need someone with you all the time who's close to you. Not a private nurse. Someone from your family or a good friend has to stay with you. I learned that poor families were usually strong and rich families frequently weak, because I could almost always get a family member to stay with a poor patient. When I had a well-to-do or upper middle class patient, I had to get a private nurse because everybody in the family was working and no one was available or willing. That taught me a great lesson about the relative strength of poor and rich families.

Of course, it most likely will not be easy to keep a friend or family member with you at all times. You have to use some muscle. When the person is told to leave, he or she must not leave. Drop the word *lawyer* quite a bit because doctors are afraid of lawyers. Say, "Well, my brother-in-law is a lawyer and he said I could stay." That sometimes works. Another technique is to bring in a bunch of tough-looking relatives. I used to take care of gypsies on the South Side of Chicago. One day the prince of the gypsies fell out of a window and hurt his head. He survived, of course, and did very well. But he was brought to the hospital by his father, the king of the gypsies, and about two hundred other gypsies. They came in a caravan of cars, all with the little flags on the aerials. It was quite a dramatic sight. All the cars pulled up, and the gypsies got out on the front lawn. About twenty of them went up with this kid to his room. Visiting hours were long over, but there wasn't one nurse or doctor who was going to go in there and tell those gypsies to leave.

The first responsibility of the friend or relative is to make sure that you are well-fed. If you expect to survive your hospital stay without starving, you have to take responsibility for your own nutrition. If the hospital food is not up to your standards, you should have food brought in from home. (If the hospital food *is* up to your standards, either you're in an exceptional hospital or you should seriously reexamine your dietary habits.) Your relative has to be prepared to run interference for you when the nurse or technician tries to interrupt or cancel your meal for a test or some other procedure. In the event that you're too weak or uninterested to feed yourself, your friend is there to feed you. He or she also can monitor your meals and tell the doctor what you've been eating and not eating. If you're on a special diet, he or she can make sure the food is part of the recommended diet.

Your friend or relative has to know what pills you're supposed to get, so that you don't get pills that the patient in the next bed should have gotten. Your partner also can make sure you're not mistaken for the next patient when they come to collect him for his surgery. Your partner can make sure you don't disappear: He or she can go with you for laboratory tests and examinations. If you're taken for x-rays, he or she can go with you to make sure you are brought to the right place, to see to it that you don't sit in a drafty hallway most of the day, to make sure you get the right x-rays.

Your partner is there to ask questions and, in general, to make trouble. Your partner should ask the nurse how fast the intravenous drip should be dropping, so that you don't get it too fast. He or she also should make sure they don't put a patient with a contagious disease in the same room.

Your partner should ask the doctor to wash his hands before he touches you. One of the side effects of doctors not making house calls is that they don't wash their hands anymore. I remember when I made house calls, people would politely say when I walked in the door, "Doctor, the bathroom is right this way." They would show me to the washroom where there was a towel and a bar of soap. It was expected that I would wash my hands before I went in to see the patient. I didn't really learn to wash my hands until I started making house calls. Now, if you watch a doctor going from room to room and patient to patient, sometimes he washes his hands and sometimes he doesn't. Sometimes he passes his hands through the water ceremoniously, but not in a way that does any good. Your partner should make sure the doctor washes his hands thoroughly before touching you. Who knows what he's had his hands in before getting to you!

If for nothing else, it's a good idea to have a partner in the hospital to protect you from the psychological dangers, the "voodoo curse" of the hospital stay. A friend or a relative provides an invaluable link to your real life, to your identity, and to your dignity that can keep you alive and strong when the hospital staff and procedures gang up on you. Even the best hospitals are frightening and dangerous. It's really common sense to have a good friend or a relative there to defend you and support you when you most need it. If you are fortunate enough to have someone who will team up with you to cause the nurses and staff to complain that the two of you are uncooperative and trouble makers, then I know that you are well-protected—and loved.

5
Holy War on the Family

If you were set on destroying the family, you couldn't do a better job than Modern Medicine. That the family *is* disintegrating has been common knowledge for years. One child out of every six is now raised by a single adult. Every other marriage is doomed.

We've even debased the word "family" itself. When *I* say family, I mean the entire collection of blood relatives: children, mothers, fathers, grandparents, aunts, uncles, and cousins. By referring to this as the "extended" family, we attempt to ignore the harm done by having only one family in twenty living with more than two adults under the same roof. On the other hand, the experts gave us the term "nuclear family" to evoke all the positive images once associated with nuclear energy. That image never was any good. What's supposed to be at the core of the atomic family? The parents? The children? Nothing? Calling the family "nuclear" prepares us for the explosiveness and instability that characterizes atoms in nature. When the nuclear family starts spinning off its individual members we can feel that it's actually *fulfilling* its destiny rather than frustrating it.

Schools and teachers are sometimes blamed for the destruction of the family, but although teachers and educators are surely part of the army of professionals attacking and crippling our families, the generals are the *doctors*. The doctors are the real leaders because without their sanction, without the blessings of Modern Medicine, none of the family-destroying agencies could *exist*, let alone succeed. Furthermore, Modern Medicine's own Holy War on the family is more devastating and vicious than the schools' ever *could* be.

Family medicine, for example, should mean the *healthy influence of the family*. To the doctor, however, family medicine is the necessary *intervention* in the family by the doctor for sacramental purposes. Any influence the family might have is less than secondary: it's useless and to be avoided. Most people think doctors stopped making housecalls because they could see more patients in the office. The real reason is that doctors don't want to meet the family on its own turf. Not only can you cram more patients into an office, but you can isolate a person from the family's influence. It's that much harder for a doctor to control the situation and dissolve family ties when he's a guest in your house.

For his "medicine" to succeed, the doctor must impose his ethics and beliefs in place of the family's. He has to take over roles traditionally played by family members. Not only don't doctors share feelings, cultural traditions, and loyalties of family members, they also don't *care* what happens. If the patient dies, it's not a tragedy, because he or she is a *patient*—not a son or daughter or mother or father or uncle or aunt or cousin. Doctors are carefully taught to distance themselves from their patients.

This distancing comes in handy when the doctor has to step in at times of crisis or stress and "take over." All religions institute sacraments or rituals at certain stressful moments in life that overwhelm us with mystery and tease us with hints of what life's all about, moments such as birth, coming of age, marriage, and death. Where other religions design these rituals to *support* the family, the Church of Modern Medicine aims only to disrupt.

I've already talked about what a dangerous place the hospital is. Modern Medicine has such arrogance that the hospital platoon is called the hospital *"family!"* No other modern religion gets away with what the Church of Medicine does routinely. No modern religion requires blood sacrifices, yet to get *married* with the doctor's sanction you have to give blood. Blood tests before marriage have little more than ceremonial value. As soon as any process becomes routine, nobody pays any attention to it. Labs make so many mistakes, most doctors don't even bother to check the results. In one study, a lab intentionally sent back positive reports for venereal disease. Very few doctors repeated the test.

That blood sacrifice before a family is even allowed to begin is only a relatively innocuous symbol of the sinister rituals to come. When the *third* member of the family enters the picture, the campaign intensifies. Now, where other religions are satisfied with reasonably unobtrusive ceremonies, Modern Medicine mounts a full scale attack by *inventing a crisis* out of a normal situation. By treating childbirth as a disease, the obstetrician makes his intervention *indispensable.* If obstetricians acknowledged the fact that more than ninety-five percent of births proceed entirely without complications, more than ninety-five percent of their services would be recognized as unnecessary. That would mean a lot fewer obstetricians—as well as healthier families.

Instead, what we have is childbirth taking place in an operating room. Of course, it may not be a bad idea to have all hospital births occur in an operating room, since hospital births are a lot more dangerous. Babies born in the hospital are six times more likely to suffer distress during labor and delivery, eight times more likely to get caught in the birth canal, four times more likely to need resuscitation, four times more likely to become infected, and thirty times more likely to be permanently injured. Their mothers are three times more likely to hemorrhage.

Whereas primitive cultures make birth an event for the whole family to share in some useful way—even to the point of allowing the husband or the mother to assist at the delivery—modern medicine allows only the doctor and his assistants to attend. "Reforms" such as birthing rooms, husbands in the delivery rooms, and prenatal discussions of what the mother-to-be wants and doesn't want are little more than marketing come-ons. Once the obstetrician has you on his turf, he's in control. He demonstrates—or flaunts—his control by putting the woman through a series of debasing maneuvers. First she must have her vaginal area shaved, though it's been known since the 1930s that doing so prior to delivery in no way decreases and may well *increase* the number of bacteria present. Then the woman must put her feet in stirrups and assume a supine position again only to satisfy the doctor's will. The intravenous fluid connection to the woman's body ensures that the doctor can rapidly administer anesthetics when *he* decides they're necessary. Already separated from her family and her control over her body (the doctor may even have decided *when* the event is to occur), the mother-to-be may be denied the *experience* of the event by being drugged senseless and memoryless. Of course, the doctor may be "forced" to put her to sleep in order to perform his *coup de grace:* the Caesarean delivery.

One of the side effects of a Caesarean delivery sometimes doesn't show up for weeks or months after the birth: babies delivered this way seem to be more likely to become victims of child abuse. Mothers who give birth this way usually are unable to be with their babies during the earliest hours and days of life because it sometimes takes that long for the effects of the anesthesia to wear off. They're also uncomfortable from the surgery itself. Not only are the first important periods of maternal-infant bonding mangled by the procedure, but whatever feelings the mother does come away with are sullied by her disappointment and pain.

Of course, mothers who give birth normally or to premature babies also are entitled to have their first few vital hours and days with their new babies unsullied. Unless a new mother puts up a hell of a fight—something not too easy to do after labor, delivery, episiotomy, and anesthesia—her baby is immediately swept away to that concentration camp known as the newborn nursery.

Hospital regulations further isolate the family from the birth experience. Visiting restrictions break up the family by allowing the new mother only one or two visitors at a time. I don't know of a more divisive situation than having to choose among husband, mother, mother-in-law, father, father-in-law, aunts, uncles, and cousins. In addition, the hospital almost *never* permits sibling visitors, and when it does, it's from the other side of a glass partition. So much for togetherness!

Pediatricians are as determined as obstetricians to weaken the family. They start by making the new mother feel absolutely unequal to the task of looking after the welfare of her baby. Before the doctor even appears on the scene, the stage for submission is set by a platoon of pediatric nurses who incessantly badger the mother with dos and don'ts regarding every aspect of the baby's care. Of course, they're only following orders.

The first broadside the pediatrician delivers to the new mother-child relationship is his "advice" regarding the feeding of the infant. As if God made a mistake in not filling her breasts with Similac, the new mother is told that man-made formula is every bit as good for the baby as her own breast milk. Early in my own pediatric training I was taught that if a mother questioned whether she should breastfeed or bottlefeed, the proper answer is: "The decision is strictly up to you; I will assist you in whatever method you decide to use."

Of course, that answer is an outright lie. Bottlefeeding—the grandaddy of all junk food—wasn't then, isn't now, and never will be "as good as " breastfeeding. Human milk is designed for human babies, cow's milk for calves. The structure and composition of each is suited to the particular needs of the intended recipient. Among animals, switching milk sources—say, for example, giving a calf sow's milk—results in sickness and, often, death for the newborn.

The bottlefed human baby is substantially more likely to suffer a whole nightmare of illnesses: diarrhea, colic, gastrointestinal and respiratory infections, meningitis, asthma, hives, other allergies, pneumonia, eczema, obesity, hypertension, atherosclerosis, dermatitis, growth retardation, hypocalcemic tetany, neonatal hypothyroidism, necrotizing enterocolitis, and sudden infant death syndrome. From a scientific, biological standpoint, formula feeding cannot be considered an acceptable alternative to breastfeeding—especially since more than ninety-nine percent of new mothers are perfectly capable of doing it.

Even premature infants should get breastmilk. When I had my

pediatric training more than twenty-five years ago, I was strongly (and thankfully) influenced by one of the great nurses in the field of premature babies, Evelyn Lundeen. Miss Lundeen not only encouraged but *insisted* that mothers supply breastmilk to their premies, even to those who weighed only two pounds. I can remember watching husbands deliver the bottles of milk their wives had pumped. There's no doubt in my mind that the premature infant fed breastmilk does much better than the premature infant fed formula. In my own practice I have discharged from the hospital many babies who weighed less than five pounds, all breastfed, of course, since now I won't accept a child as a patient unless the mother is determined to breastfeed.

Telling mothers that breastfeeding is superior to formula feeding is my recipe for eliminating a pediatric practice. If a pediatrician tells a mother the truth that breastfeeding is good and bottlefeeding is dangerous, it will lead to feelings of guilt on the part of the mother who chooses not to breastfeed. The guilty mother then will scurry off to a pediatrician who's willing to relieve that guilt by telling her that it makes no difference whether or not she breast-feeds. On the other hand, those women who do breastfeed will have babies that never get sick. There goes the pediatric practice!

You won't find many pediatricians who insist that a woman breastfeed her baby. Instead, you'll find what I call Pediatric Doublethink, the statement that breastfeeding is best, but formula is *just as good.* You'll find pediatricians who hand out free sample six-packs of infant formula to new mothers; you'll find pediatricians who insist that newborns waste their sucking reflex and energy on sugar-water bottles; you'll find pediatricians who push free "supplementary formula" kits on mothers who are breastfeeding; and you'll find pediatricians who discourage a mother from breastfeeding if her baby doesn't gain as much weight as the manual provided by the formula company says it should. You'll find pediatricians neglecting to inform mothers that infant formula can contain from ten to 1,000 times as much lead as breastmilk; neglecting to tell a mother that breastfeeding protects her infant from all infectious diseases she has had or fought off through her immune system; neglecting to tell mothers that breastfeeding promotes better bone maturation and intellectual development; and neglecting to tell them that breastfeeding will help protect the mothers themselves from cancer of the breast.

Breastfeeding is better for the *family,* too. The bond between a mother and her child is secure and healthy when the mother breastfeeds. Not only does the sucking of the infant stimulate hormones that reduce postnatal bleeding and discomfort and cause the uterus to shrink back sooner, but it also gives the mother sensual pleasure as well. Bottlefeeding, however, gives the mother no such pleasure. It does make possible—indeed *necessary*—the sacred four-hour feeding schedule, which does untold damage to all involved, in the name of "regularity."

Leaving the hospital and going home with her new baby doesn't protect the mother and family from the divisive onslaught of doctors. The parting advice of the pediatrician and nursery staff is likely to be something like, "Remember, if the baby cries, let him or her cry it out because crying will strengthen its lungs, and besides you want it to learn not to cry when it wants something." Now this piece of advice—besides flying in the face of common sense—ignores the instincts not only of the baby, but of every mother I've ever talked to. God apparently made another mistake in having babies cry when they want something!

All the way down the line the doctor uses his authority to put the family at odds with its own instincts and traditions. Instead of trusting in the wisdom of accumulated experience, the family loses confidence in its own feelings and submits before the doctor's "education," his "certified wisdom" signified by his diploma and specialty papers. If you ask the doctor where it's written that a male pediatrician who may never have fathered a child and certainly never mothered one is a better source of information about the needs of a crying baby than the baby's own mother or grandmother, he'll most likely point to the framed diplomas on the wall.

Even though the young mother may spend only a few minutes a month with the pediatrician, a gang of experts endorsed by the doctor—such as Doctors Spock, Salk, Ginott, and Bettelheim—are prepared to confuse her thoroughly through the varying opinions in their books and articles. The young mother is totally without a defense against this barrage of advice since she has no confidence in her own thoughts and feeling and since she has been taught by the doctor(s) to reject her mother's and grandmother's advice as "old wives' tales." Instead, she turns to the old doctors' tales and is left with her head spinning!

Since few American families live with or close to other relatives, the mother is *physically* removed from the solace and support her mother or grandmother could provide. My recipe for making a mother at least neurotic and at worst crazy is to put her in the house alone eyeball to eyeball with a new baby with only a gaggle of disagreeing experts to guide her through the crises of her first few months as a mother. This situation—which is the most common one in this country—can make a woman neurotic before the baby's a year old. (A father in the same situation wouldn't last a month.) Since there's no one to help her *in* the home, the woman tries to save herself by escaping *from* the home. In many cases, the strain on the husband and the wife is so great when they have only each other to look to as both the cause and the solution of their problems, that the marriage ends in divorce. Or, less drastically, the woman wastes no time finding a "fulfilling" job outside the home. Either way, the child is shunted off to a day-care center.

A woman's vision of fulfillment in a job outside the home is more often than not an illusion. Most jobs—including those performed by men—are not fulfilling in the least, but rather are dull, routine, mechanized tasks that mean only one thing: a paycheck. Few jobs are as fulfilling as homemaking and childrearing. Women do need and should cultivate activities inside and outside the home that will help them fulfill their personal identity. But precious few paying jobs do that. Even with the best of jobs, a working woman often finds herself juggling her many roles and finds that she has little or no time left for the things she cares about most. Not only must she work, but she also must adopt the goal-oriented attitude of men who compete for success, an attitude which in itself is unhealthy— for men *or* women.

The goals of working outside the home may be illusory, but

the effects on the family are real. Whereas children used to leave the home at age six, with day-care centers sprouting and mothers filling them as soon as they're allowed, we now have children "starting school" as early as age one! By day-care center I don't mean the old fashioned nursery school in which a child spent only a few hours. Meals were not served in nursery schools, and the child spent most of the day at home. Not so in today's day-care center.

In Europe, day-care centers often are located in the same factories, shops, or offices as the mothers' jobs, or at least close enough so the mother can lessen the impact of separation by visiting the child and sharing meals. In this country, however, day-care centers are located too far away for mother and child to share any more than a quick goodbye before mother hustles off to get to work across town and returns tired and grouchy eight, nine, or maybe even ten "fulfilling" hours later.

At the day-care centers, the child is fed by strangers, not by its mother. What is meant by nature to be a subtle mechanism in which a child is nurtured by his or her family becomes instead a situation where the child is influenced at a crucial period in its development by strangers. Of course, to apply the veneer of education to the child's separation from the family, we now have academic departments dedicated to certifying experts in "early childhood education."

Many day-care centers provide breakfast, lunch, and dinner. I can remember most elementary schools twenty years ago had no facilities for feeding their students, but today school lunches are now a matter of course in every school district. Since lunches are now served on the premises, lunch periods have been shortened to prevent even the children who *want* to go home for lunch from doing so, even if mom *is* home. What we end up with is a situation in which the child spends more and more of his or her time with people who most likely don't share the same values, traditions, or ethics as the family. Since the children spend less and less of their most important developmental time with their family, they grow up truly "independent" of all, for better or worse, that their family holds dear—and of the *family* itself.

All of this wouldn't be possible if doctors didn't sanction and encourage unhealthy notions of "independence." I'm reminded of the story of a young New York family. The husband told me that his wife had gone back to work when he had lost his job, but that he had just gotten another job. His wife was going to continue to work, but in a new job as director of a seven-story day-care center. Their three-year-old son was attending the same center. I told the father that I thought this was a good arrangement, since the child would have his mother reassuringly close to him all day. "Oh no," gasped the father, "I don't want him to be reassured. I want him to be independent." The father and mother had ensured their son's independence to the point of mapping out separate bus routes for mother and child on the way to the center.

I can't help wondering whether that father may not someday regret making his son so independent. After all, isn't dependence the proper business of a three-year-old? Behind that foolish young man I see a pediatrician somewhere, urging him to encourage independence among family members—starting with the "let him cry it out" admonition—while *discouraging* his independence from the *doctor's* intrusion in the family's responsibilities. The dependence between a mother and her child is the core and the model for a family's health-producing interdependence. Family members are *supposed* to depend on one another! We should celebrate a Family Declaration of Dependence *every day*.

When a child goes off to school, Modern Medicine enlists the help of teaching professionals to keep the family at bay. Not only is the parent's role as teacher usurped, but the parents are shunted off into meaningless activities such as PTA bake sales and carnivals. Parents are removed from the arena where the real battle for their children's minds is taking place. Clever tactics such as changing styles of teaching—new math for one generation, old math for the next—keep parents from playing a significant role in their children's education. They can't even help with the homework! Sex education the children receive in school more likely than not conflicts with the family's values. PTA meetings take the parents away from the family in the evenings. The kids start staying away more and more to attend extracurricular activities. Little by little, the gap between parents and children is widened.

When it comes time to deal with problems, parents are too confused and distant from their children to be effective. They've been robbed of any confidence they might have had at the beginning. Off to the psychiatrist! They've been successfully recruited for psychotherapy or the ministrations of some other chamber of the Church of Modern Medicine.

This new team of experts gives the family just what it needs to solve its problems: a vocabulary. Parents are given a bag of words with which to describe their children: irresponsible, immature, hostile, resentful. Children are given a bag of words to describe their parents: inhibited, repressed, over-protective, rejecting. Needless to say, these words are tossed about between family members like brickbats. Rather than giving the family tools for repairing relationships, stock definitions freeze the thinking processes in which people can come to understand each other.

By nature, psychiatry is family-divisive. Psychiatrists encourage people to say bad things about their relatives. If conducted properly, such therapy can release tensions between and within people and allow greater emotional mobility and health. But very little of it that's going on is very well conducted, because I see a lot of people going in for therapy and very few people coming out any better. How can you come out any better when the psychiatrist has you pegged even before you open your mouth? If you arrive for your appointment late, he'll say you're hostile. If you're early, you must be anxious. And if you're right on time, you're compulsive! You can't win! When I see a married couple go to a psychiatrist for family counseling, I can predict with pretty good horse racing odds that they will end up getting a divorce.

The platoons of "helping professionals" that gang up on the family are *disabling*. They offer few tools to help a family stay together. Because they rob the family of its own tools, the family is left with no effective resources. It's no wonder that by the time the children reach college age they can't wait to get away from the house. Who

would want to live in a house where the people were virtually un-
equipped to relate to one another in any way other than the
mechanized, subject-to-the-whims-of-psychiatry fashion advised by
magazine experts?

Nowadays, a college education is somehow less than it should be
if the student doesn't attend a college at least a day's travel from
home. Everybody, ideally, goes to school on the opposite coast.
Midwesterners have two coasts to choose from. This wide separation
between family members removes any vestiges of influence and
leaves the child totally "free" to be influenced by peers and professors. If someone could show me how this does any good for either
parents or children, I'd let the subject drop. In my experience, I see
a higher rate of illness among first-year college students than almost
any other social subgroup. They are more prone to depression,
hypothyroidism, tuberculosis, rheumatic fever, infectious mononucleosis, and menstrual disturbances. And, small wonder, their
suicide rate is second only to that of American Indian children sent
away from the reservation for high school.

None of this would be possible without the sanction of Modern
Medicine. From one end of life to the other, the Church interferes
and substitutes its empty ceremonies for the bonds and traditions of
the family. Life is debased. As soon as you allow a single natural
process to be corrupted or "improved" by treating it as if it were a
disease, the whole organism of living processes can begin to rot.
Children once performed useful functions within the home. Nowadays their usefulness is related entirely to outside activities. The
same fate awaits people when they reach old age. Older people are
treated with contempt and swept out of the home into retirement
"resorts" or rest homes. Why should they stay around the house?
Their advice isn't respected, nor are their special talents and skills
developed over a lifetime. Modern Medicine would much rather
have old people separated from their families, their talents, and
their respect. That way, they provide a much better potential patient population. They get sick more often under the voodoo curse
propagated by the Church, the curse of unavoidable debility in old
age, the curse of the long steady decline to death. Not only is the

person isolated from the family at the last moments of life, strapped and wired into the Intensive Care Unit, but sedatives and tranquilizers handed out by the family doctor at the funeral rob mourners of any emotional release they may get from crying. Even *there*, Modern Medicine, ever on guard against disruptive behavior, dulls the senses to rob participants of precious moments in their lives.

As Modern Medicine gets stronger, more forceful methods are used to attack the family. You have to submit to the Church in order to go to school. They won't let you in the door unless you can prove that you've received all the sacramental immunizations. Sooner or later doctors and some school districts are going to get really rough and go after people who refuse to have their children immunized. They'll simply declare the children victims of child abuse and remove them from the home.

This sort of violence already is going on. Lately, I've been involved in more and more cases in which my function as a physician has been to spring children from hospitals. The usual story is this: The child has a temperature of 103 or 104 and may have a throat or ear infection. He's taken to the hospital where the doctor sees that he's got a couple of bruises on his body. The social worker is called in, and after a few questions the finger is aimed at the parents. The child is hospitalized, presumably for his own protection. Then the parents have to find somebody who will testify that there is no possibility of child abuse and that the bruises are from some other cause.

At one time, child abuse was obvious to doctors. It consisted of children who came in with multiple broken bones. Today, that definition has been extended so that if you take a child into the emergency room and he or she has a few bruises, you're immediately questioned by a social worker. With the thousands of empty beds in hospital pediatric units, it's to everybody's advantage—except the family's—to try to establish a charge of possible child abuse.

A mother I know had a baby and decided to leave the hospital right away because she didn't like the hospital and she wanted to breastfeed her baby. She went home and about a month later came back for a checkup at the hospital outpatient clinic. Her baby hadn't gained enough weight. The doctor said this was because of the breastfeeding and told her to stop breastfeeding immediately and put her baby on formula. She decided she didn't want to do that, so she continued to breastfeed. At the next month's checkup—I don't know why she went back!—the baby had gained more weight but not as much as the doctor thought the baby should. He said it was a possible case of child neglect and ordered the baby hospitalized.

The mother called her friends in the La Leche League who had been advising her with her breastfeeding. They got in touch with me, since I am a medical advisor to the League. I looked into the case and found that the woman had been doing a very good job of breastfeeding. What she was most concerned about now was that they wouldn't let her stay with the child. By the time I was contacted, the child had been away from the mother for five or six hours. Her breasts were filling up. She was getting uncomfortable, but the hospital didn't care. They were feeding the infant formula. Things were reaching an urgent point, so I got in touch with the State's Attorney and within an hour the mother was allowed to go upstairs and nurse the baby. Next morning, an emergency hearing was held and the child was released.

This sort of thing is not a rare incident. As long as Modern Medicine aids the State by sanctioning the State's attack on the family, the State lets Modern Medicine have all the power it needs to enforce its laws. I now warn parents to be extremely careful when they bring their children to a hospital emergency room because you never know what can happen once a doctor starts to examine a child.

I wonder whether certain elements of American society haven't *always* been out to kill the family. The very *existence* of America split millions of families around the world as the great waves of immigration filled our cities. Many of these immigrants, however, depended on relatives already here to help them over the difficult first months in the New World. The pioneer families certainly had to stick together, too—although, once again, the initial leap into the wilderness generally split young parents and children from their older relatives who stayed behind. Since older relatives—bearers, as well as symbols, of traditions carried over from "the old country"—weren't around to maintain the traditions, subsequent generations lost touch with the "old ways" of doing things. The melting pot wasn't a melting pot at all: it was a sterilizing cauldron in which family ties and traditions were boiled away. When immigration was cut off after World War I, the stage was set for the war against the family to begin in earnest. Without fresh supplies of immigrants to maintain ties with families and their traditions, people could at last start not only to escape those traditions but to forget that they ever existed.

Modern Medicine took advantage of this situation to boost the development of pediatrics, my own specialty. During the first four decades of this century pediatrics had no more than a few thousand practitioners. But when World War II started, the country needed women in the factories to take the place of men who had to go and fight. There was no way these women were going to be able to do that and take care of their children the way they had before the war. Oh, nurseries *could* have been set up in the factories, to allow the mothers to do their patriotic duty and their biological duty as well. But instead, doctors simply *denied* the biological duty. The words "baby-sitter," "nuclear family," and "mother surrogate" came into fashion during the war. Instead of saying that every child needed a mother, doctors said that every child needed a mother *or* a mother surrogate. That way, millions of Rosie the Riveters could join the war effort without a twinge of guilt over leaving their children in the care of strangers.

Since these mothers couldn't be with their babies for more than a couple of hours at the end of each day, breastfeeding became impractical. It didn't become any less biologically necessary or superior as far as the baby's health was concerned. But since it was impractical, doctors pronounced formula feeding to be not only the answer to a dilemma, the better of two evils (the alternative evil being not feeding the baby at all), but the *equal* of the only scientifically sound alternative.

Like the priest who "blessed" the hot dogs to save parishioners from the moral bane of eating meat at a Friday night church carnival, doctors gave their blessing to bottle feeding. Had they told the truth, they would have advised women that all studies showed a higher mortality rate among bottlefed babies. They would have told women the benefits of breastfeeding over bottle feeding. They might have, patriotically, thrown up their hands and admitted the dilemma while giving women the opportunity to make an informed choice. But they chose instead to subvert biology in favor of politics and power. They, in effect, told women they didn't have to be responsible to biology, to nature's laws. While pediatrics grew in popularity and power, manufacturers of infant formulas—some of whom also make drugs—grew into multinational super-corporations.

Modern Medicine has teamed up with these corporations to export the technology of infant nutrition all over the world. Actually, what they're doing is carrying on human infant sacrifices among vast numbers of people who have no way of defending themselves. In 1952, ninety-five percent of Chilean mothers breastfed their children beyond the first year. By 1969, only six percent did, and only twenty percent of the babies were being nursed as long as two months. This decline in breastfeeding—and similar declines across the world—has been brought about by doctors allowing salesmen from the formula manufacturers to go into the maternity wards and sell mothers on the "modern" way to feed your baby. Of course, free samples are distributed. Doctors carefully advise mothers that formula is as good or better than their own milk. No mother wants to be accused of being old fashioned when her baby's health is at stake, and especially when the formula salesperson wears the same white coat that the doctor wears.

Many of these new mothers—in fact *most* of them—can't afford the extra cash to pay for infant formulas. They also may not have facilities for preparing the formula correctly. Nestle's baby book says, "Wash your hands thoroughly with soap each time you have to prepare a meal for baby." Formula also has to be mixed with clean water. Now in the United States or Europe, where every household has three or four sinks connected to a reasonably clean water supply, these directions present no problem. But in the underdeveloped countries where formulas are most aggressively marketed, it's a different story. In one investigation in Chile, eighty percent of the bottles examined had high bacterial contamination. In Malawi's capital city, sixty-six percent of the households have no washing facilities at all.

Furthermore, by the time the free sample runs out, the mother's breasts are dry and her pocketbook empty. She can't buy more formula, so she may end up feeding her infant *worse* food. When we brag that our infant mortality rate is among the best in the world (which, for all our bragging, it isn't), we should stop and think about the role Modern Medicine plays in keeping infant mortality rates in underdeveloped countries artificially high.

Modern Medicine attacks the family for the simple reason that if you want to convert someone to a different religion, you first go after his family ties. *Don't listen to your mother or your grandmother. Those are old wives' tales. Listen to us.* We are taught not to depend on anyone but the professionals—the doctors. With the family influence gone, what I call the vertical transmission of values from one generation to the next is gone, too. All you're left with is horizontal transmission of values through the influence of peers and other contemporary sources of information such as research studies, news media, and the entertainment-advertising industry. And doctors.

Health maintenance organizations (HMOs) are a good example of the kind of medical institution that thrives on the breakdown of the family. In an HMO, people pay a set fee every month and have virtually unlimited use of the Church's "health maintaining" facilities. Besides the fact that those facilities' ability to maintain health is most doubtful, the fact is that the *family itself* is the best health maintenance organization there is! *Where* do HMOs flourish? Where families have little influence. Ask Henry Kaiser, who set up his Kaiser-Permanente HMO in California, where there are no *families* because everybody's moved there from somewhere else. If you want to set up an HMO elsewhere in the country, you've got to go to a university where, again, people have no families because the students *and* the faculty are all from elsewhere. Or you set one up in a slum neighborhood, where family stability and size is also at a minimum. You will have a lot of trouble setting up an HMO in an area where family ties are strong. Not only do family members find the best doctors and stick to them, but families tend to keep their members healthier without the benefit of a gaggle of professionals, thank you.

Of course, Modern Medicine is out to destroy the family for precisely that reason. Strong families obviate the need for doctors and other "helping" professionals. It's no accident that prostitution is called the oldest *profession* rather than the oldest *business*. Unlike business transactions, which are characterized by an exchange of commodities, professionals give *themselves* in the performance of a service in return for a fee. More often than not, that service is one which ideally would be performed by a family member, friend, or by the person himself. The prostitute replaces the wife, as the doctor replaces the entire constellation of the family. The weaker the family, the greater the opportunity for professionals. A healthy society is characterized by strong, positive family relationships and subsequent *minimal need for doctors*. Modern Medicine's Holy War on the family is a battle for survival against a competing system of health and healing. As long as the enemy is anything that can build, maintain, or restore health, the casualty will be the individual welfare of every defenseless person who goes to a doctor.

To protect your family against the attacks of doctors and other "helping" professionals, you first should recognize that experts seldom have a better idea of what's "right" than you do. This becomes quite plain when you look at what the experts were claiming was gospel truth in the past. For example, the standard pediatrics texts during the early 1920s advised: "The practice of playing with infants and exciting them by sights, sounds, and motions until they shriek with apparent delight is often harmful and should be condemned. Never hug and kiss them. Never let them sit on your lap. If you must, kiss them once on the forehead when they say goodnight. Babies under six months old should never be played with. And of kissing, the less the better. Rocking is forbidden. So are pacifiers. Should the child attempt to pacify himself by sucking his thumb, pasteboard splints must be applied to his elbows to prevent him from bending his arms. At night his arms must be tied to his sides."

Of course, we "know" now that this advice was ridiculous. But I wonder how many mothers went against their natural inclinations to entertain and stimulate their babies and as a result raised families of dullards.

If you are thinking about starting a family, you can begin by *deciding for yourself* how many children you want to have. Don't accept the advice of zero population growth advocates, or any other self-proclaimed expert on the ideal size of a family. I know of no evidence that suggests that children from large families are any less successful than children from small families. You shouldn't allow political considerations to determine the size of your family.

When you do start your family, find a doctor who is qualified to deliver your baby at home. Home birth eliminates all the risks of a hospital stay and allows you to spend the time immediately following your family's addition enjoying yourself rather than defending yourself against the intrusions of the hospital staff. If you find your obstetrician trying to talk you out of home birth by listing dangers *before* he's examined you, he's obviously not qualified. A qualified home birth doctor or midwife will support your desire to have your baby at home and will carefully examine you to determine whether you are subject to any special risks that make home birth especially dangerous. For the vast majority of families, there is far less risk in a home birth than in a hospital birth.

If you are unable to find a doctor who will perform a home delivery (at the end of the book I list resources for this search), you should go for the next best thing, which is a hospital delivery followed by a quick exit for home. Barring any serious complications, there is no reason why you and your baby can't leave the hospital as soon as you feel able—which can be anywhere from twenty minutes to a few hours. My favorite story regarding a family's reaction to a doctor hostile to home birth involves a former student of mine. When his wife told the obstetrician she wanted her husband present during the delivery, the doctor said he felt the delivery of a baby was far too personal an event for a husband to be there. She shot back that if it was *that* personal she wasn't so sure she wanted the doctor to be there either! They did go ahead and have their first baby in the hospital, but they left twenty minutes after the baby was born. Their subsequent babies have been delivered at home, and the husband has become a specialist and a leading authority on home birth.

Since Modern Medicine begins its assault on the family by separating husband from wife during the birth of the baby, you should insist on a delivery in which the husband is present. Of course, he should not merely suit up and stand around. He's there to assist, support, and protect his wife and child.

At all points along the way you should learn to identify and question rules that separate families. After the baby is born, for example, the nurse will take him or her away unless you make known before, during, and after the birth that you want the baby in your arms or your husband's *immediately*. Your baby is yours, not the hospital's. Keep him or her close to you for those important minutes after birth.

Even if the hospital promises rooming-in, you should be aware that hospitals sometimes revoke the privilege without warning. At one hospital, rooming-in disappears every year when the hospital's regular pediatric nurses leave for the summer!

Next you must protect yourself and your baby against your doctor's prejudice against breastfeeding. Here, again, you are going to have to learn to lie to the doctor. When he says bottle feeding is just as good as breastfeeding, you won't get anywhere by arguing with him, and you might make him especially vindictive against your particular effort. The best thing to do is to just nod ambiguously and ignore him. An acquaintance of mine was told by her doctor that her baby wasn't gaining weight fast enough. He gave her a free six pack of formula and told her to supplement her breastfeeding with it. She didn't argue with him, but on her way home the formula ended up in the first trash can she came across.

More than twenty years ago, when a Chicago-area woman named Marian Tompson had her first baby, she could find no one to go to for advice about breastfeeding. Her doctor didn't know the first thing about breastfeeding. So she and six other women started a group called La Leche League, whose purpose is to teach mothers how to breastfeed their children. Since its founding, La Leche

League International has helped hundreds of thousands of women throughout the world, not to mention the children of these mothers. For support and encouragement in breastfeeding, join La Leche League.

There are a number of "little" things that doctors tell women they should do with their babies which I believe are detrimental to the family. First, they tell them breastfeeding is OK, but that solid food should be given after six weeks. This is nonsense. There is no need to give a baby solid food before six *months*. The six-week rule results in a daily slapstick routine in which the mother tries to jam, ram, or cram something, *anything,* that faintly resembles "solid" food into the baby. There is no better food for the baby than mother's milk.

Don't be afraid to pick up your baby when it cries. If he or she didn't need you, he wouldn't be crying. The idea that a baby should be "trained" not to cry for its parents by ignoring it is patently absurd, and it ignores instinct. If the baby wakes up during the night, perhaps it needs the extra security that sleeping in the same room—or even the same bed—as mom and dad would give. The rule that children and parents must sleep in separate rooms is one of those rules that separate families for all the wrong reasons. I don't know many *adults* who are really comfortable sleeping alone. How can you expect an infant who has known the warmth and intimacy of its mother's body to adjust to the cold, empty dark of "its own room."

When you do start to feed your baby solid food, ignore the propaganda of the baby food manufacturers—who never seem to run out of university research centers that will run a study proving that home-prepared food is less healthy than the processed stuff they put in jars. If the food you eat at home is truly less healthy than baby food in jars, your whole family is in trouble. Feed your baby what you eat. Chop it, grind it, puree it, or blend it. Be careful to introduce only one new food at a time, however, so as to catch any developing allergic reactions as soon as they begin.

Try to make mealtimes a shared experience. This means getting the whole family at the table at once. When family members are together for a nice meal, they are automatically encouraged to talk and share themselves with one another.

Stay as close to relatives as you can. Try especially to keep elderly relatives close by, because they need you *and* you need them. Invite relatives to babysit. The more relatives a child is close to and comfortable with, the better.

Avoid separation whenever possible. Mothers and fathers should insist on staying with their children in the hospital. Also, consider alternatives to day-care. A job at home, when all factors are considered, may be more fulfilling than work outside the home. If a full-time or part-time job outside the home is necessary, try to set up an arrangement with relatives or with neighbors. You might be able to start up a cooperative nursery school among your neighbors. A home-type environment is superior to the institutional setting of the day-care center. If your job or school keeps you and your children separated during the day, don't participate in organizations that meet in the evening when you should be spending time with your family.

Spend holidays with relatives, friends, and neighbors. Psychiatrists almost never take vacations around Christmas, because the season is marked by great depression and a heightened suicide rate among their patients. Holidays were made for people to get together and celebrate and renew the bonds that have supported them throughout their lives. People who have allowed the war against the family to keep them apart from their family are natural victims of frustrated legitimate needs.

Visit your college-aged children who are away from home. Encourage them to come home when their schedule permits and sometimes when it doesn't. Make sure they know that you're there when they need you, because they *will* need you. Colleges are becoming increasingly competitive, lonely places.

All along the way you have to learn to deal with professionals. Sometimes this means you have to be practical rather than pure. For example, assume that your doctor will bully you if you let him, especially if you are a woman. Now this is certainly not the way things *should* be. But as long as things *are* that way, I advise people, especially women, to go to the doctor in pairs. Wives should go with their husbands, since a doctor will pay more attention to a woman's problem if the husband is along. Sure, doctors *shouldn't* treat women as second-class humans; but they do, and you shouldn't sacrifice your health for an abstract principle. We need successful heretics, not martyrs.

A more humorous—and less politically charged—situation where you have to be more practical than pure is when your child goes off to nursery school. I remember a mother phoning me at 11:00 one night to tell me she had an emergency. When I asked her the nature of the emergency, she said her three-year-old boy wasn't toilet trained yet and couldn't enter nursery school until he was. When I asked her why this was an emergency, she told me she lived on the eighteenth floor of a high-rise apartment and was going to jump out the window if I couldn't give her any advice. I agreed it was an emergency.

I have long advised mothers to send their non-toilet trained children to nursery school after lying to the school and saying the child is trained. Many children do, quite mysteriously, become toilet trained on the first day of school. In the case of the others, the teacher usually calls the mother after a week of frustration and says, "I thought you told me the child was toilet trained!"

The mother's reply should be: "What have you done to my child?"

Sometimes in dealing with doctors, nurses, and other professionals, you have to be downright *indomitable.* Or *immovable,* as the case may be when a nurse tries to remove you from the bedside of a hospitalized relative. First of all, terminally ill relatives should be allowed to die at home. Hospitals don't own people at either end of life. If a relative is in the intensive care unit, you have to buck the ten minute rule to remain with him or her. Your first move should be simply to stand still. Don't enforce the hospital's rule for them. When the nurse asks you to leave, ask why. If she says your presence is too much of a strain on the patient, tell her that you are a better judge of whether your relative is strained by your presence. Then challenge the nurse to produce evidence. She may then retreat to a new position: the rules say you have to leave. Ask for a copy of the rules in writing. Her next move will be to summon the doctor. Ask him the same questions. How do you know my presence here causes a strain on my relative? How do you know that the presence of hospital staff is automatically good and the presence of family members automatically bad for the patient?

While you're protecting your family against Modern Medicine's Holy War, recognize that besides being protected, the family should be *used* as a health resource. At times of crisis, seek out the advice and support of family and friends. When other members of the family need help and support, *be there*. Because if you're not, you can be sure that the doctor will, soon enough.

6
Doctor Death

Modern Medicine is an idolatrous religion, for what it holds sacred are not living things but mechanical processes. It doesn't boast of saving souls or lives but of how many times this or that new machine was used and how much money was taken in by the process.

What resides at the core of every religion, the core from which hope radiates when all human attempts to deal with earthly conditions fail, is the Deity, the One Who Transcends it all. To get to the core of Modern Medicine you have to wade through an ocean of man-made drugs and fight your way through endless tons of machinery. If you then don't understand why the Church is savagely idolatrous and must be destroyed, you will when you stare its Deity in the face.

The God of Modern Medicine is Death.

In fact, a new word was recently coined by Dr. Quentin Young to describe one activity of Modern Medicine: iatrogenocide. Iatrogenocide (iatros is the greek for doctor) is the systematic destruction of a large group of people by *doctors*. An example of iatrogenocide is the infant sacrifices in developing countries, which I described in the preceeding chapter. This widespread marketing of infant formula among people who can't afford it or implement it safely amounts to a doctors' crusade against unsuspecting, defenseless infidels.

How truly deadly the Church is comes into stark relief whenever there's a doctors' strike. In 1976 in Bogota, Colombia, there was a fifty-two-day period in which doctors disappeared altogether except for emergency care. The "National Catholic Reporter" described "a string of unusual side effects" from the strike. The death rate went down thirty-five percent. A spokesman for the National Morticians Association said, "It might be a coincidence but it *is* a fact." An eighteen percent drop in the death rate occurred in Los Angeles County in 1976 when doctors there went on strike to protest soaring malpractice insurance premiums. Dr. Milton Roemer, Professor of Health Care Administration at UCLA, surveyed seventeen major hospitals and found that sixty percent fewer operations were performed. When the strike ended and the medical machines started grinding again, the death rate went right back up to where it had been before the strike.

The same thing happened in Israel in 1973 when the doctors reduced their daily patient contact from 65,000 to 7,000. The strike lasted a month. According to the Jerusalem Burial Society, the Israeli death rate dropped fifty percent during that month. There had not been such a profound decrease in mortality since the last doctors' strike twenty years before! When the doctors were asked to explain this phenomenon, they said that since they only attended emergency cases, they could invest their best energies into the care of the truly ill people. When they didn't have to listen to the day-to-day, presumably unimportant complaints of the average patients, they could devote themselves to a greater saving of life.

That's not such a bad answer. I've been saying right along that what we need is a perpetual doctors' "strike." If doctors reduced their involvement with people by ninety percent and attended only emergencies, there's no doubt in my mind that we'd be better off.

We just can't get away from the fact that a disturbing amount of doctors' energies are devoted to death-oriented activities. I tell my students that to succeed in Modern Medicine all you have to do is look for some field that encourages death or thinking about death and you've got a brilliant future ahead of you. As far as Modern Medicine is concerned, death is a growth industry. You can't pick up a medical journal without reading the latest on: contraception, abortion, sterilization, genetic counseling and screening, amniocentesis, zero population growth, "death with dignity," "quality of life," and euthanasia. All of these activities have as their purpose the prevention or termination of life. Things such as mass genetic screening and compulsory amniocentesis with the option of abortion are now merely at the talking stage, but talk is a prelude to action.

In our rush to embrace these activities—with enthusiasm I can describe only as religious fervor—we are duped into both ignoring their dehumanizing effects and their lack of scientific justification. They are sacraments, after all. Sacraments of death.

For example, thanks to Modern Medicine's sanction, what were once called sins are no longer sins at all. Thus, homosexuality is now called an "alternative lifestyle." This and other forms of non-procreative sexual activity are encouraged, promoted, indeed glorified. In my lifetime I've seen society's attitudes towards masturbation, for example, go through three distinct phases. When I was young, masturbation was sinful and dangerous. It either made you blind or grew hair on your palms. Of course, scientists didn't even *try* to determine whether or not this was true. Later, when I was in college, masturbation was neutral, it was neither harmful nor good. Now, however, we're in the third phase of masturbation. Not only is masturbation OK, but it's normal, healthy, and good. If you *don't* do it, there's something wrong with you. And if you don't *know how* to do it, there are people who will *teach* you—especially if you're a woman.

I explain this radical shift in attitude within the space of a generation by relating it to society's attitude towards population. When having children was good, masturbation was less than good. When the tide turned and having children became bad, masturbation, homosexuality—and *anything else* that helped us not to have more children—became good.

We *are* programmed for life very deeply in our natures. Our strongest urges are procreative and life-supporting, but these are the instincts and activities that Modern Medicine *attacks*. Thus, dangerous forms of birth control—abortion on demand, masturbation, and homosexuality, all non-procreative forms of sexual activity —result in diminution of population growth. These "alternative lifestyles" which do not promote life are acceptable, but things people have been doing for thousands of years to *promote* life are not.

The only "alternative lifestyle" that is not acceptable is any one which precludes participation in the Church. It's a sin if you have your baby at home, but not a sin if you have an abortion. It's a sin if you honor a foreign god by going to a chiropractor, but it's not a sin if you go to one of the shrines of Modern Medicine for a sex change. Any biological stress these activities may have on the body and soul are ignored.

What is wrong here is that the Church exaggerates its encouragement of non-life activities while it exaggerates its contempt for life. The common sense, more human, approach is trampled. Modern Medicine, for example, says that any woman should have the right to an abortion. Whether or not this is politically beneficial, it's important to recognize that *biologically* there may be more to it than simple freedom of choice. Some traditional ethical systems, such as Jewish law, *mandate* abortions when the life of the mother is at stake. A judgment is made that the life of the mother is more important than the life of the infant. But in the way Modern Medicine encourages abortion, it doesn't consider life at all, either the mother's or the infant's—its main interest is its own technology.

One of the sacred catastrophes of the past twenty years is the Church's promotion of birth control *at all costs*. Here the difference between a moral "sin" and a biological "sin" is most clear. Birth control, *per se*, is not morally wrong. Certain methods of birth control, however, are *biologically* wrong in that their effects on the life of the user are negative. Short of refusing to deal with harmful methods such as the Pill and the IUD, if doctors acknowledged to every woman the real dangers involved and allowed every woman to make an informed choice, there would be little problem. But doctors *never* allow a patient to choose or not choose a procedure based on a balancing of the biological risk with how much a woman wishes to endanger her life. They simply ignore biology; they ignore the fact that a particular procedure may do more harm than good. So profound is their devotion to this ignorance, the only explanation is that the deep purpose of Modern Medicine is being loyally served through it.

When I was a medical student in the late 1940s and early 1950s, I thought medicine was concerned almost exclusively with saving and prolonging life. I hardly remember any serious discussion about what is now referred to as "the quality of dying." I learned to treat death by denying it, by maintaining hope. Denial is supposed to be a bad word nowadays, despite the fact that a number of research studies show that patients with cancer and other serious diseases seem to live longer when they deny and fight their disease than when they "accept" it. In the *British Medical Journal* (November 22, 1975) there appeared this tidbit: "Evidence from research certainly supports the view that psychological factors can play a part in determining the length of survival. Weisman and Worden recently compared patients with cancer who survived for longer than survival statistics would suggest with others whose death occurred sooner than predicted. They found that motivation to survive, as expressed in 'rising resentment' as the illness progressed and a positive attitude to treatment, was associated with longer survival. Conversely, patients who expressed a wish to die or a ready acceptance of death died sooner than expected. Similarly, several studies suggest that patients with coronary thrombosis who are prone to depression or become depressed after an infarction are less likely to survive than those who are not melancholic. All in all it seems that attitudes of determination and hope prolong life, whereas acceptance of death or attitudes of gloom and despondency shorten it."

I was recently at a medical meeting at which a doctor who treats cancer patients with chemotherapeutic agents admitted that as interested as he was in saving lives and in discovering new methods of treatment, he was even more interested in making sure his patients' deaths occurred with a certain degree of "acceptance and peace." He and his staff spend a major part of their time and resources counseling dying patients, preferably in the absence of their families. It's no mystery to me why these Salesmen of Death insist on "counseling" patients in the absence of the patient's family. The family's whole *purpose*, and therefore its *influence*, is for *life*, not death.

This doctor—and many like him who make a study of death—operate under the assumption that a person should accept death. In effect, they "treat" the patient to death, since they can't treat him or her to life. They assert that denying death is in some way mentally unhealthy. Thanatologists claim that if you don't talk about death, face it, and resign yourself to it, you'll make yourself sick!

As far as I'm concerned, thanatologists and everyone else who counsel resignation to death have it backwards. A doctor who tells a patient that there's no hope for his or her life is not doing that patient any good at all. First of all, the doctor is making an enormous assumption in presuming his power is the only one that can restore the patient's health. Telling a patient he or she is going to die is tantamount to a curse. The patient believes it, so it comes true.

We are just beginning to find out how the mind can affect the body's own healing powers. Of course, doctors will be the last to acknowledge that the body has significant power to heal itself. But you can see how preserving optimism should be the first priority. Rather than pronouncing the patient's doom, the doctor should help the patient plan his or her future. It's one thing to inform a patient that he or she suffers from a deadly disease and that the magic of the doctor doesn't go far enough to do any good. But it's another thing entirely to tell a patient that the end is inevitable.

Of course, if the doctor were to admit that he had no power over the patient's affliction but that *other powers*—such as those of other healers or the patient's own—may, he would lose his control over the patient. Furthermore, since Modern Medicine's rites are not only growing less and less successful but also more and more deadly, it makes good business sense to prepare the patient for the inevitable results of the doctor's work. Once death is accepted as "just another part of life," it can be given its proper place on the hospital menu.

Modern Medicine is now better geared for killing people than it is for healing them. You see this best at both ends of life, where life is more delicate and death is closer and easier to ascribe to "natural causes." It's becoming increasingly dangerous, for instance, for a Mongoloid newborn with an intestinal obstruction to reside in a nursery. Though the obstruction is surgically correctable, there is an increasing likelihood that he will be deprived of care and allowed to die. The same goes for retarded children in state hospitals who are unfortunate enough to fall seriously ill.

At the other end of life, "undesirables" are allowed or even encouraged to die. Old people in nursing homes, despite the flowery advertisements accompanying these places, are put there to keep them out of "real" people's way. They're put there to die, and they generally take the hint. It doesn't take much to recognize a curse when it's directed at you.

Doctors actually encourage old people to get out of the way and die. Their attitudes towards old people and their problems amount to a sentence of long, slow death. Such phrases as, "You'll just have to learn to live with it," and "What do you expect at your age?" tell the old person that his or her problems are to be *expected*. Consequently, old people expect them. And *get* them. Because the doctor doesn't admit that the problems usually associated with old age are not inevitable at all and that they can be prevented or dealt with naturally, the patient is wide open for the whole array of palliative—and deadly—drugs. In cultures not yet under the death swoon of Modern Medicine, people live to advanced age in full possession of their capacities. But Modern Medicine renders old people *incapable,* and rather than prolonging their lives, it just makes dying longer and harder.

I've always believed that if you want to find out what a society's really all about, look at its mottoes and what it claims to prohibit. Look on a coin and you'll see "In God We Trust." Now if there's a society that trusts *less* in God than the United States, I haven't heard of it. The motto of the medical profession has always been "First Do No Harm." As we've already seen, that motto is respected more in the breach than anywhere else, but it serves a very useful purpose. The medical profession can hide a lot of atrocities under the guise of doing no harm.

The first thing to change when one cultural force overcomes another and takes over a society is *language*. When you control a people's way of describing things, you control their way of dealing with them.

We have a population "explosion," which makes a lot of babies sound ominous and harmful. We have pregnancy "planning" or pregnancy "termination" to make abortion sound clinically detached from life and death. We say "euthanasia" instead of "mercy killing," which somehow was too accurate a description even with the nice adjective. The most outrageous attempt to hide reality by changing vocabulary is the term "death with dignity." Now, death is all right under any circumstances as long as it's with "dignity." The funny thing is that in the situations in which this term is most often employed, the act of "pulling the plug" removes all possibility of dignity from the event.

To me, all these death-oriented activities are frighteningly reminiscent of the Nazis. The medical profession in Germany drifted into these same activities prior to World War II. German doctors willingly got rid of "useless people" such as severely retarded and deformed children. Liberalized abortion and euthanasia were followed by the "death with dignity" of old people—meaning they were allowed and encouraged to die. Later came the murder of gypsies; then the rounding up of anti-Nazis and Jews. The Nazis were fighting a Holy War, too.

As Modern Medicine's War on Life intensifies, hospitals are rapidly becoming unable to handle the overload. So we have to build "death centers" called—again, using a very comfortable-sounding word to hide the reality—*hospices*. Death counselors are also moving into hospitals, which I've already identified as Temples of Doom, to prepare patients for the institution's major product. Of course, this is nothing if not good marketing strategy. What you have to do to sell anything is create a *desire* and an *acceptance* of your product. Since the product of Modern Medicine is death, we are "softened" to the *idea of non-life* first. Once we are alienated from our own instincts for life, accepting dehumanizing, dangerous procedures is easier. Finally, with only a purgatory of drug-induced semi-life to look forward to, we welcome the salesmen of death when they come to counsel us out of this world.

When that moment comes, the full attention of the Church is directed at your participation in the Central Mystery. Like the Catholic Mass, which celebrates the Resurrection, your death in the intensive care unit is the supreme sacrament. So sacred are the preliminary ceremonies that you are separated from your family, just as I'm sure sacrificial victims of earlier religions were kept apart from relatives who might interfere with the machinations of the priests. Instead of holding the hand of a family member, you're connected to the finest and most advanced electronic gadgetry. At last, deep within the Temple's Holy of Holies, you fulfill the Promise and commune with the God of Modern Medicine.

When a new religion wants to discredit an old religion, it does so by blaming the problems of the people on the old gods. Modern Medicine says your disease is caused by a virus. Who created the virus? The old God. And so on. It's not you or we who are causing your disease, it's natural things such as viruses and bacteria and the tendency of cells to divide irregularly and heredity and . . . . The old God is responsible—the God of Life.

Modern Medicine can free you from the bonds of the old God. Modern Medicine can give you a new God that can counteract all the pesky forms of life that get in the way, such as bacteria, viruses, cells dividing out of control, inconvenient fetuses, deformed or retarded children, and old people.

Fortunately, the same natural processes that Modern Medicine attacks appear to have the weight of history on their side. If you examine the major religious groups that have survived the longest—the Jewish, Christian, Moslem and Oriental religions—all have ethical systems which are not too different. They favor large families and respect of older generations by younger—within limits, of course. All judge a society by its treatment of marginal groups such as premature babies, retarded children, and old people. They discourage non-procreative forms of sexual activity. Of course, there are differences among them, but not as formidable as their differences from religions that are death-oriented and which haven't survived. Ancient Greek and Roman religions favored population control, abortion, infanticide, killing of old people, homosexuality and other non-procreative forms of sex—all in the name of quality of life.

Yet quality of life is very simply a function of quantity of life. The reason I'm interested in long life is that I hope to have many grandchildren. The quality of my life depends on how many grandchildren I get to see grow up. I want to live as long as I can. If I'm truly *alive* as long as I'm living, then the quality of my life will take care of itself. I won't need a gang of professionals around to counsel me on the quality of my life.

Of course, the professionals—led by the doctors—are aggressive in their intrusion into the quality *and* quantity of our lives. What we need to do is find doctors who are life-oriented, doctors who share our regard for life and who use their intelligence and skills to protect it.

That, unfortunately, may be the hardest job of all.

7
The Devil's Priests

I always laugh when someone from the American Medical Association or some other doctors' organization claims that doctors have no special powers over people. After I finish laughing, I always ask how many people can tell you to take off your clothes and you'll do it.

Because doctors are really the priests of the Church of Modern Medicine, most people don't deny them their extra influence over our lives. After all, most doctors are honest, dedicated, intelligent, committed, healthy, educated, and capable, aren't they? The doctor is the *rock* upon which Modern Medicine's Church is built, isn't he?

Not by a long shot. Doctors are only human—in the worst ways. You can't assume your doctor is *any* of the nice things listed above, because doctors turn out to be dishonest, corrupt, unethical, sick, poorly educated, and downright stupid more often than the rest of society.

My favorite example of how doctors can be less intelligent than the situation calls for is a matter of public record. As part of the hearings before the Senate Health Subcommittee, Senator Edward Kennedy recalled a skiing injury to his shoulder, suffered when he was a young man. His father called in four specialists to examine the boy and recommend treatment. Three recommended surgery. The advice of the fourth doctor, who did not recommend surgery, was followed, however. He had just as many degrees as the others. The injury healed. Senator Kennedy's colleagues then proceeded to question Dr. Lawrence Weed, Professor of Medicine at the University of Vermont and originator of a highly popular patient record system for hospitals. Dr. Weed's reply was that the "senator's shoulder probably would have healed as satisfactorily if the operation had been performed."

When doctors are formally tested, the results are less than encouraging. In a recent test involving the prescribing of antibiotics, *half* of the doctors who voluntarily took the test scored sixty-eight percent or lower. We've already seen in the previous chapters how dangerous it is to have a doctor work on you. All of that danger doesn't necessarily derive from the inherent risks of the treatment itself. Doctors simply botch some of those procedures. When *I* meet a doctor, I generally figure I'm meeting a person who is narrow-minded, prejudiced, and fairly incapable of reasoning and deliberation. Few of the doctors I meet prove my prediction wrong.

Doctors can't be counted on to be entirely ethical, either. The dean of Harvard Medical School, Dr. Robert H. Ebert, and the dean of the Yale Medical School, Dr. Lewis Thomas, acted as paid consultants to the Squibb Corporation at the same time they were trying to persuade the Food and Drug Administration to lift the ban on Mysteclin, one of Squibb's biggest moneymakers. Dr. Ebert said that he "gave the best advice I could. These were honest opinions." But he also declined to specify the amount of the "modest retainer" Squibb Vice-President Norman R. Ritter admitted paying both him and Dr. Thomas. Dr. Ebert later became a paid director of the drug company and admitted to owning stock valued at $15,000.

In 1972, Dr. Samuel S. Epstein, then of Case-Western Reserve University, one of the world's authorities on chemical causes of cancer and birth defects, told the Senate Select Committee on Nutrition and Human Needs that "the National Academy of Sciences is riddled with conflict of interest." He reported that panels that decide on crucial issues such as safety of food additives frequently are dominated by friends or direct associates of the interests that are supposed to be regulated. "In this country you can buy the data you require to support your case," he said.

Fraud in scientific research is commonplace enough to keep it off the front pages. The Food and Drug Administration has uncovered such niceties as overdosing and underdosing of patients, fabrication of records, and drug dumping when they investigate experimental drug trials. Of course, in these instances, doctors working for drug companies have as their goal producing results that will convince the FDA to approve the drug. Sometimes, with competition for grant money getting more and more fierce, doctors simply want to produce results that will keep the funding lines open. Since all the "good ol' boy" researchers are in the same boat, there seems to be a great tolerance for sloppy experiments, unconfirmable results, and carelessness in interpreting results.

Dr. Ernest Borek, a University of Colorado microbiologist, said that "increasing amounts of faked data or, less flagrantly, data with *body English* put on them, make their way into scientific journals." Nobel Prize winner Salvadore E. Luria, a biologist at the Massachussetts Institute of Technology, said "I know of at least two cases in which highly respected scientists had to retract findings reported from their laboratories, because they discovered that these findings had been manufactured by one of their collaborators."

Another now classic example of fraud occurred in the Sloane-Kettering Institute where investigator Dr. William Summerlin admitted *painting* mice to make them look as though successful skin grafts had been done. A predecessor to Dr. Summerlin in the field of painting animals was Paul Kammerer, the Austrian geneticist, who early in the twentieth century painted the foot of a toad in order to prove the Lamarckian theory of transmission of acquired traits. When he was later exposed in Arthur Koessler's book, *The Case of the Midwife Toad,* Kammerer shot himself.

Dr. Richard W. Roberts, director of the National Bureau of

Standards, said that "half or more of the numerical data published by scientists in their journal articles is unusable because there is no evidence that the researcher accurately measured what he thought he was measuring or no evidence that possible sources of error were eliminated or accounted for." Since it is almost impossible for the average reader of scientific journals to determine which half of the article is usable and which is not, you have to wonder whether the medical journals serve as avenues of communication or confusion.

One method of judging the validity of a scientific article is to examine the footnote for the source of funding. Drug companies' records regarding integrity of research are not sparkling enough to warrant much trust. Doctors have been shown not to be above fudging and even fabricating research results when the stakes were high enough. Dr. Leroy Wolins, a psychologist at Iowa State University, had a student write to thirty-seven authors of scientific reports asking for the raw data on which they based their conclusions. Of the thirty-two who replied, twenty-one said their data either had been lost or accidentally destroyed. Dr. Wolins analyzed seven sets of data that did come in and found errors in three significant enough to invalidate what had been passed off as scientific fact.

Of course, research fraud is nothing new. Cyril Burt, the late British psychologist who became famous for his claims that most human intelligence is determined by heredity, was exposed as a fraud by Leon Kamin, a Princeton psychologist. It seems that the "coworkers" responsible for Burt's research findings could not be found to have actually existed! There is even evidence that Gregor Mendel, father of the gene theory of heredity, may have doctored the results of his pea-breeding experiments to make them conform more perfectly to his theory. Mendel's conclusions *were* correct, but a statistical analysis of his published data shows that the odds were 10,000 to one against their having been obtained through experiments such as Mendel performed.

Doctors' unethical behavior is not limited to the medical business. A doctor whose name is practically synonymous with the development of a major surgical procedure was convicted of five counts of income tax evasion for omitting more than $250,000 from his tax returns for 1964 through 1968. A few years ago the chairman of the Board of the American Medical Association was indicted, convicted, and sentenced to eighteen months in jail after pleading guilty to participating in a conspiracy to misuse $1.8 million in bank funds. According to the FBI, he and his codefendants had conspired to "obtain unsound indirect loans for their own interest ... paying bank funds on checks which had insufficient funds to back them ... and defrauding the government...."

Keep in mind that these shenanigans are going on at the highest levels of the medical profession. If this kind of dishonesty, fraud, and thievery is going on among the bishops and cardinals of Modern Medicine at Yale and Harvard and the National Academy of Sciences and the AMA, imagine what is going on among the parish priests at the other medical schools and medical societies!

Perhaps the most telling characteristic of the profession that is supposed to deliver *health* care is that doctors, as a group, appear to be sicker than the rest of society. Conservative counts peg the number of psychiatrically disturbed physicians in the U.S. at 17,000 or one in twenty, the number of alcoholics at more than 30,000, and the number of narcotics addicts at 3,500 or one percent. A thirty-year study comparing doctors with professionals of similar socio-economic and intellectual status found that by the end of the study nearly half the doctors were divorced or unhappily married, more than a third used drugs such as amphetamines, barbiturates, or other narcotics, and a third had suffered emotional problems severe enough to require at least ten trips to a psychiatrist. The control group of non-doctors didn't fare nearly as badly.

Doctors are from thirty to one hundred times more likely than lay people to abuse narcotics, depending on the particular drug. At a semiannual meeting of the American Medical Association in 1972, surveys cited showed that nearly two percent of the doctors practicing in Oregon and Arizona had been disciplined by state licensing authorities for drug abuse. An even larger percentage got into trouble for excessive drinking. Even the AMA admits that one and one-half percent of the doctors in the United States abuse drugs. Various reform and rehabilitation measures over the years have not changed these percentages. Keep in mind that these figures represent only the identified cases. In Illinois, for example, Dr. James West, chairman of the Illinois Medical Society's Panel for the Impaired Physician, reported that four percent rather than two percent of Illinois doctors are narcotics addicts. He further estimated that eleven-and-one-half percent were alcoholics—one in nine.

Suicide accounts for more deaths among doctors than car and plane crashes, drownings, and homicides *combined*. Doctors' suicide rate is twice the average for all white Americans. Every year, about 100 doctors commit suicide, a number equal to the graduating class of the average medical school. Furthermore, the suicide rate among female physicians is nearly four times higher than that for other women over age twenty-five.

Apologists for the medical profession cite several reasons for doctors' high rate of sickness. The drugs are easily available to them; they must work long hours under severe stress; their background and psychological makeup predisposes them to stretch their powers to the limits; and their patients and the community make excessive demands on them. Of course, whether or not you accept these reasons, they don't explain away the fact that doctors *are* a very sick group of people.

Nonetheless, I prefer to look for more reasons. Fraud and corruption in the research process comes as no surprise to anyone who witnesses the lengths to which drug and formula companies go to lure doctors to their way of thinking. Free dinners, cocktails, conventions, and subsidized research fellowships still are only superficial explanations. When you examine the psychological and moral climate of Modern Medicine, you begin to get closer to understanding why doctors are so unhealthy.

Medical politics, for example, is a cutthroat power game of the most primitive sort. I much prefer *political* politics, because there you have the art of the *possible*, which means you have to compromise. Medical politics is the art of sheer power. There is no compromise: you go right for the jugular vein before your own is torn out. There's no room for compromise because churches *never* compromise on canon law. Instead of a relatively open process in which people with different interests get together to try to get the most out of the situation that they can, in medical politics there is a rigid authoritarian power structure which can be moved only through winner-take-all power plays. Historically, doctors who have dared to change things significantly have been ostracized and have had to sacrifice their careers in order to hold to their ideas. Few doctors are willing to do either.

Another reason why doctors are less prone to compromise is because doctors tend to restrict their friendships to other doctors. Close friendships between doctors and non-doctors are nowhere near as frequent as among other professions. Consequently, doctors rarely have to defend their opinions among people who don't share their background and who might offer a different point of view. Doctors can develop their philosophy in relative privacy, foray at intervals into the public scene to promote these ideas, and then rapidly retreat to the security of other doctors who support the views of the in-group. This luxury is not available to others in influential positions in public life.

Of course, doctors do see their patients. But they don't see them as people. The doctor-patient relationship is more like that between the master and the slave, since the doctor depends on the complete submission of the patient. In this kind of climate, ideas can hardly be interchanged with any hope of the doctor's being affected. Professional detachment boils down to the doctor rendering the entire relationship devoid of human influences or values. Doctors rarely rub elbows with non-doctors in any other posture but the professional.

Furthermore, since the doctor's ambitions project him into the upper classes, that's where his sympathies lie. Doctors identify with the upper class and beyond, even. They view themselves as the true elite class in society. The doctor's lifestyle and professional behavior encourage autocratic thinking, so his conservative politics and economics are predictable. Most doctors are white, male, and rich—hardly in a position to relate effectively with the poor, the non-white, and females. Even doctors who come from these groups rarely return to serve and "be with" them. They, too, become white, male, and rich for all practical purposes and treat their fellows with all the paternalistic contempt other doctors do.

When asked where doctors learn these bad habits, I used to reply that doctors learned them in medical school. Now I realize they learn them much earlier than that. By the time they get to premedical training, they've picked up the cheating, the competition, the vying for position—all the tricks they know they need if they want to get into medical school. After all, our university system is modeled after the medical schools, and our high schools are modeled after our universities.

The admissions tests and policies of medical schools virtually guarantee that the students who get in will make poor doctors. The quantitative tests, the Medical College Admission Test, and the reliance on grade point averages funnel through a certain type of personality who is unable and unwilling to communicate with people. Those who are chosen are the ones most subject to the authoritarian influences of the priests of Modern Medicine. They have the compulsion to succeed, but not the will or the integrity to rebel. The hierarchy in control wants students who will go through school passively and ask only those questions the professors can answer comfortably. That usually means they want only one question at a time. One of the things I advise my students to do in order to survive medical school is to ask one question but never ask two.

Medical school does its best to turn smart students stupid, honest students corrupt, and healthy students sick. It isn't very hard to turn a smart student into a stupid one. First of all, the admissions people make sure the professors will get weak-willed, authority-abiding students to work on. Then they give them a curriculum that is absolutely meaningless as far as healing or health are concerned. The best medical educators themselves say that the half-life of medical education is four years. In four years half of what a medical student has learned is wrong. Within four years of that, half again is wrong, and so on. The only problem is that the students aren't told which half is wrong! They're forced to learn it all. Supervision can be very close. There is no school in the country where the student-teacher ratio is as low as it is in medical school. During the last couple of years of medical school, you frequently find classes of only two or three students to one doctor. That doctor has tremendous influence over those students, through both his proximity and his life-and-death power over their careers.

Medical students are further softened up by being maliciously fatigued. The way to weaken a person's will in order to mold him to suit your purposes is to make him work hard, especially at night, and never give him a chance to recover. You teach the rat to race. The result is a person too weak to resist the most debilitating instrument medical school uses on its students: fear.

If I had to characterize doctors, I would say their major psychological attribute is fear. They have a drive to achieve security-plus that's never satisfied because of all the fear that's drummed into them in medical school: fear of failure, fear of missing a diagnosis, fear of malpractice, fear of remarks by their peers, fear that they'll have to find honest work. There was a movie some time ago that opened with a marathon dance contest. After a certain length of time all the contestants were eliminated except one. Everybody had to fail except the winner. That's what medical school has become. Since everybody can't win, everybody suffers from a loss of self-esteem. Everybody comes out of medical school feeling bad.

Doctors are given *one* reward for swallowing the fear pill so willingly and for sacrificing the healing instincts and human emotions that might help their practice: *arrogance.* To hide their fear, they're taught to adopt the authoritarian attitude and demeanor of their professors. With all this pushing at one end and pulling at the other, it's no wonder that doctors are the major sources of illness in our society. The process that begins with cheating on a biology exam by moving the microscope slide so that the next student views the wrong specimen, that continues with dropping sugar into a urine sample to change the results for those who follow, with hiring others to write papers and take exams, and with "dry labbing" experiments by fabricating results, *ends* with falsifying research reports in order to get a drug approved. What begins with fear and fatigue over exams and grades ends with a drug or alcohol problem. And what begins with arrogance towards others ends up as a doctor prescribing deadly procedures with little regard for the life and health of the patient.

My advice to medical students is always to get out as soon as possible and as easily as possible. The first two years of medical school are survivable because the students are relatively anonymous. The student should try his or her best to remain so, since if the professors don't know him they can't get to him. The last two years are more personal, but the student has more time off to recover from the assaults. If a student simply does enough work to pass and doesn't get all wrapped up in the roller derby mentality, he or she can make it to the finish line relatively unscathed. Then, as soon as the student is eligible for a state license, I advise him to quit. Forget residency and specialty training because there the professionals have the student day and night, and he can really be brainwashed. That's when the real making of the Devil's priests occurs.

Doctors are only human. But so are the rest of us, and sometimes we need the services of all-too-human doctors. Because the doctor-priest acts as a mediator or a conduit between the individual and the powerful forces the individual feels he cannot face alone, a *faulty* conduit can result in some very powerful energy flowing into the wrong places. For example, when doctors are compared with other people in evaluating retarded and other handicapped persons, those who always give the most dismal predictions and the lowest evaluations are the doctors. Nurses are next lowest, followed by psychologists. The group that always gives the most optimistic evaluation is the parents. When I'm faced with a doctor who tells me a child can't do certain things and parents who tell me that the child can do them, I always listen to the parents. I really don't care which group is right or wrong. It's the attitude that counts. Whatever attitude is reinforced and encouraged will prove true. I know doctors are prejudiced against cripples and retarded people because of their education—which teaches that anyone who is handicapped is a failure and is better off dead—so I can protect my patients and myself against the doctors' self-fulfilling prophecies of doom.

Yet doctors continue to get away with their attitude and their self-serving practices. Even though doctors derive a great deal of their economic status and power from insurance companies, the doctors are in control. So much in control, in fact, that insurance companies generally act against their own interests when the choice is that or weaken the power of doctors. Blue Cross and Blue Shield and other insurers logically should be searching for methods of *decreasing* unnecessary utilization of medical services. Occasionally, we see half-hearted attempts in this direction, such as the flurry of rules requiring second opinions before elective surgery, or the every-so-often policy of discontinuing reimbursement for procedures long fallen into oblivion. These efforts are more window dressing than anything else. They are introduced with considerable fanfare, rapidly generate a groundswell of controversy, and then quietly slip away. Regardless of how well-intentioned they are, they still address themselves only to the peripheral aspects of medical care and not to the areas where real money is to be saved. If insurance companies really wanted to cut costs, they would promote reimbursement for a wide range of simpler, more effective, cheaper procedures—such as home birth. And they would allow reimbursement for measures that restore and maintain health without drugs or surgery—such as diet therapy and exercise.

One of the most fascinating statistics I've ever run across is one that was reported by the Medical Economics Company, the publishers of the *Physician's Desk Reference*. Among other questions, they asked a representative sampling of more than 1,700 people, "If you learned that your doctor had lost a malpractice suit, would it alter your opinion of him?" What amazes me is that *seventy-seven percent* of the people said NO!

Now I don't really know if that means that people *expect* their doctors to commit malpractice or if they *don't care* whether he does or not!

I do know that the insurance companies are bamboozled by the doctors into spending more money than they have to. I also know that only about seventy doctors lose their licenses every year—despite all the obvious corruption, sickness, and dangerous malpractice. Here we come to one of the truly wondrous mysteries of Modern Medicine. Despite (or because of?) all that fear and competition among medical students, doctors are extremely reluctant to report incompetent work or behavior on the part of their colleagues. If a hospital, for example, discovers malpractice by one of its doctors, the most that will happen is the doctor will be asked to resign. He won't be reported to state medical authorities. When he seeks employment elsewhere, the hospital will most likely give him a shining recommendation.

When the famous Marcus twin-brother team of gynecologists were found dead of narcotics withdrawal during the summer of 1975, the news that the doctors were addicts came as a surprise to everyone but their colleagues. When the brothers' "problems" were noticed the year before by the hospital staff, the twins were asked to take a leave of absence to seek medical care. When they returned to New York Hospital-Cornell Medical Center, they were watched for signs that they had improved. They had not. Were they then whisked off the staff and kept out of touch with patients before anyone was seriously harmed? Were they reported to state licensing authorities? No. They were told *in May* that as of *July 1*, they would not be allowed to work in the hospital. They were found to have died within days after they lost the privilege to admit patients to the hospital.

Another favorite example of doctors allowing their colleagues to commit mayhem on unsuspecting patients occurred in New Mexico. A surgeon tied off the wrong duct in a gall bladder operation and the patient died. Although the error was discovered at autopsy, the doctor was not disciplined. Apparently, he wasn't taught the right way to do the operation, because a few months later he performed it again, wrong—and another patient died. Again, no punishment and no surgery lesson. Only after the doctor performed the operation a third time and killed another person was there an investigation resulting in the loss of his license.

If I had to answer the question of why doctors are so reluctant to report negligence in the practice of their colleagues yet so cutthroat when it comes to medical politics and medical school competition, I go back to the basic emotions engendered in medical school: fear and arrogance. The resentment doctors are taught to feel for each other as students is transferred to the patients when the doctor finally gets into his own practice. Other doctors are no longer the enemy as long as they don't threaten to rock the status quo through politics or research which doesn't follow the party line. Furthermore, the old fear of failure never goes away, and since the patient is the primary threat to security—by presenting a problem which must be solved, much like a medical school test—any mistake by a single doctor threatens the security of *all* doctors by chalking one up for the other side. Arrogance on the part of any professional group is always directed at the outsiders that the group fears most—never at the members of the same profession.

Obviously, doctors get away with more arrogance than any other professional group. If Modern Medicine weren't a religion, and if doctors weren't the priests of that religion, they wouldn't get away with anywhere near so much. Doctors get away with substantially more than priests of other religions, because of the peculiarly corrupt nature of Modern Medicine.

All religions promote and relieve guilt. To the extent that a religion is able to encourage useful behavior by promoting guilt and relieving it, that religion is "good." A religion which promotes too much guilt and relieves too little, or which encourages the wrong kind of behavior—behavior which will not result in the improvement of the welfare of the faithful—is a "bad" religion. An example of how a religion promotes and relieves guilt is the almost universal proscription against adultery. Obviously, if religions didn't try to make people feel that adultery was "wrong" and encourage them to feel guilty about it, more and more people would do it and necessary social structures would weaken. People wouldn't know who their parents were, property could not be orderly transferred from generation to generation, and venereal disease could threaten the existence of an especially energetic culture.

Doctors are so powerful precisely because they have, as priests of the Church of Modern Medicine, *removed* all the old guilts. Modern Medicine invalidates the old guilts which, strangely enough, held people to their old religions. Nothing is a "sin" anymore, because if there is a physical consequence, the doctor has the power to fix you up. If you get pregnant, the doctor can perform an abortion. If you get venereal disease, the doctor can give you penicillin. If you are gluttonous and damage your heart, the doctor can give you a coronary bypass. If you suffer from emotional problems, the doctor has Valium, Librium, and other narcotics to help you get by without caring, or feeling. If those don't work, there are plenty of psychiatrists.

There is one "sin" that Modern Medicine *will* make you feel guilty about: *not going to the doctor.* That's OK, because the doctor is the priest who takes away every other guilt. How much harm can there be in guilt that drives you to the doctor every time you feel sick?

The doctor-priest gets away with a lot because he can claim to be up against the very Forces of Evil. When a priest is in a touchy situa-ion and the probability for success is dismal, he escapes blame by saying that he's up against the Devil. The doctor-priest does the same thing. When the prognosis is not good, he retreats into his mortality and admits that he's only a man up against the Devil. Then, if he wins, he's a hero. If he loses, he's a defeated hero—but still a hero. Never is he seen in his true light—as the *agent* of the Devil.

The doctor never loses, though he plays both sides against the middle and takes bigger risks than necessary. That's because he has succeeded in identifying his rituals as sacred and potent regardless of their real efficacy. He uses his holiest implements to raise the ante and make the game more ominous than it really needs to be. If a mother comes into the hospital with her baby in the breech position and the fetal monitor says the baby is in distress, the doctor loses no time in declaring it a life-and-death situation—which, indeed, it becomes once he starts to perform a Caesarean-section delivery. Biologically, the doctor knows the C-section is dangerous. But the game is no longer being played by biological rules. It's a religious game, a ceremony, and the priest calls the shots. If mother and child survive, the priest is a hero. If they die, well . . . it was a life-and-death situation anyway.

The doctor never loses: only the patients lose. The adage that a doctor buries his mistakes still applies. We used to refer mistakenly to doctors as airplane pilots. If the plane goes down, the pilot goes down with it. But the doctor *never* goes down with the patient.

Doctors also escape blame by claiming that their failures are caused by their successes. If you point out, for example, that a disproportionate number of premature babies seem to be turning up blind in premie nurseries, the doctor will say that it's the price you have to pay. "Gee, we managed to save these little 1- and 2-pound babies. Of course they all end up blind and deformed. They'd be dead if we didn't save them." Doctors use the same excuse with the problem of diabetic blindness. The reason we have so much diabetic blindness, they say, is because we have succeeded in keeping so many diabetics alive longer. Doctors will use this "we managed to keep them alive longer" excuse for *every* disease they have trouble treating successfully—which includes all the major causes of non-accidental death. They absolutely ignore the biological facts that creep in and point the finger at Modern Medicine's mismanagement of both health and disease. Doctors even manage to get away with blaming *their own* disease on their successes. When you point to the large numbers of dishonest, unhappy, and just plain sick doctors, the excuse usually runs something like this: "The reason for the psychological disability is our tendency to be compulsive, perfectionistic, easily given to a sense of guilt if our clinical efforts fail." A president of the American Medical Association offered that one.

Doctors protect themselves further through the sacred language of the priest. A religion must have a sacred language to separate the discourse of the priesthood from the lowly banter of the masses. After all, the priests are on speaking terms with the powers that keep the universe on course. We can't have just *anyone* listening in. Sacred language of doctors is no different from jargon developed by any elitist group. Its main function is to keep outsiders ignorant. If you could understand everything your doctor was saying to you and to other doctors, his power over you would be diminished. So when you get sick because of the generally filthy conditions in the hospital, he'll call your infection *nosocomial.* That way, you'll not only not get angry at the hospital, but you'll feel privileged to have such a distinguished sounding disease. And too *scared* to get mad.

Doctors use their semantic privileges to make you feel stupid and convince you that they are genuinely privy to powers that you'd better not mess with. As long as their rituals are mysterious, as long as they don't have to justify them biologically, they can get away with anything. They're not even subject to the laws of logic. Doctors will, for example, justify coronary bypasses by saying that everyone who has one feels better. But if you ask to be treated for cancer with laetrile because everyone you know who has been treated with it feels better, your doctor will tell you that it hasn't been scientifically proved effective.

Semantic isolation also serves to disenfranchise the individual from the healing process. Since the patient has no hope of *knowing* what's going on, let alone *assisting,* why allow him or her any part in the process at all? The patient gets in the way of the ritual, so get the patient out of the way. That's one reason why doctors aren't interested in helping patients maintain their health. To do that, they'd have to *inform* them rather than *work on* them. Doctors aren't going to share information, because that means sharing power.

To back them up, doctors have an enormous tonnage of technological gadgets which proliferates alarmingly. First of all, the patient must stand in awe of the array of machinery the doctor assembles to attack his problem. How could any single person—other than the doctor, who has the *power*—hope to control such forces? Also, the electronic wizardry adds weight to the doctor's claim that he "did everything he could." If it's just a doctor standing there with a black bag, "all that he could" doesn't mean very much. But if the doctor throws the switches on $4 million worth of machinery that fills three rooms, that means he did "all that he could" and then some!

Typical of any developed religion, the ceremonial objects in which the most power is concentrated reside in the Temple. The higher the status of the temple, the more machinery within the walls. When you get to the cathedrals and the little "Vaticans" of Modern Medicine, you are up against priests who have the weight of *infallibility* behind them. They can do no wrong, so they are the most dangerous.

The reforms that have been introduced in an effort to solve some of the problems I've talked about in this chapter don't impress me as doing very much good. Rehabilitation programs, for example, don't really attack the roots of the sicknesses doctors seem to fall prey to. That may be a result of their shying away from exposing the problem as a disease of the *core* of Modern Medicine. Of course, doctors are not trained to attack the core of *any* problem, merely to suppress the symptoms.

Attempts to keep doctors' knowledge up-to-date also do little good, since what doctors *don't* need is more of the same kind of information they received in medical school. That's precisely what they get in most continuing medical education programs. They're taught by the same people who taught them in medical school. Who's responsible for keeping *them* properly informed?

As I've already said, you have to protect yourself. To do that, you need to remember the two major attributes of doctors: fear and arrogance. What you have to do is learn how to work on his fears without challenging his arrogance until you have the winning hand. Since doctors are scared of you and what you can do to them, you shouldn't hesitate to use that fear. Doctors are scared of lawyers, not because lawyers are so powerful but because lawyers can ally themselves with *you*, whom the doctor *really* fears. If a doctor does you dirty, sue him. It is in courts and juries that you're most likely to find common sense. Find a good lawyer who knows a lot about medicine and who is not afraid to put a doctor through the ringer. If there's one thing a doctor doesn't like it's to be in court on the wrong end of a lawyer—because that's one place where the patient has allies that can effectively challenge the doctor's priestly immunity. The increase in malpractice suits is encouraging, since it means more and more people are being radicalized to the point where they challenge the doctor's power to determine the rules.

If your doctor gives you trouble but not enough to take him to court, you need to be careful about how much you challenge him—not because of what he can or cannot do to you, but because *how far* you go will determine your effectiveness. If a doctor threatens you and becomes angry, you should stand up to him. Don't back down. Threaten him back. When a person really threatens a doctor, the doctor almost always backs down if the person shows that he means it. Doctors back down all the time because they figure, "What do I need this one kook for?"

It's important, though, not to threaten a doctor unless you are prepared to carry through. In other words, don't reveal your rebellion until you have to, until you have the emotional commitment and the physical capability to carry on a successful campaign. Don't get into an argument with a doctor with the hope of changing his mind on anything. Never say to the doctor who's treating you for cancer with traditional chemotherapy, "Doc, what do you think about laetrile?" You won't get anywhere, and you won't get any laetrile, either. Don't say to the doctor who recommends a security bottle for your baby, "But I'm breastfeeding and I don't want to do that." Don't bring your doctor columns from the newspaper expecting him to change his mind or try something new. Don't challenge him until you're ready with an alternative action. Do your own homework.

What does a Catholic do when he decides that his priests are no good? Sometimes he directly challenges them, but very seldom. He just leaves the Church. And that's my answer. Leave the Church of Modern Medicine. I see a lot of people doing that today. I see a lot of people going to chiropractors, for example, who wouldn't have been caught dead in a chiropractor's office a few years ago.

I see more and more people patronizing the heretics of Modern Medicine.

8

If This Is Preventive Medicine, I'll Take My Chances with Disease

A fellow doctor once wrote and asked me how the medical profession "might play an inspirational and practical role in the quest for world peace."

My answer was: "Go out of business."

We've already seen what a disaster curative medicine has become, but so-called preventive medicine is just as dangerous. In fact, the juggernaut of Modern Medicine's drive for power over our lives is preventive medicine. It's no secret what mayhem power-hungry institutions—including governments—can get away with hiding behind the intention of "preventing" trouble. Modern Medicine gets away with even *more*. For example, the Defense Department explains the billions it spends by forwarding the old "we're protecting you from camels" routine. Though a great portion of those billions is no doubt wasted money, at least the Defense Department can point to the virtual absence of camels as evidence that *some* of the money is spent on worthwhile activities.

Modern Medicine can't even make that claim. There's no way

anybody can justify the billions of dollars we spend every year on "health care." We're not getting healthier as the bill gets higher, we're getting sicker. Whether or not we have national health insurance is, at best, irrelevant and, at worst, one of the most dangerous decisions facing us in the years ahead. Because even if all doctors' services were free, disease and disability would not decrease.

I wonder if we can really expect anyone to ask whether more of what we already have too much of will do us any good. Modern Medicine has succeeded in teaching us to equate *medical care* with *health*. It is that equation which has the potential to destroy our bodies, our families, our communities, and our world.

We've already seen how much of what Modern Medicine describes as "preventive" medicine is not only ineffective but dangerous. The sacrament of the regular physical exam exposes you to the whole range of dangerous and ineffective procedures. From this "act of faith" you receive the absolution of the priest—if you're lucky. First you have to give him a full confession, a complete and honest history including things your wife and best friends don't even know. Then he'll pass the ceremonial stethoscope over your vital parts—a stethoscope that has a good chance of not working properly. The doctor will check your orifices, further the humiliation by having you give a bottle of urine to the nurse, hit you ceremoniously on the knee with a rubber hammer, and pronounce you saved!

Or write out your penance in Latin.

Or—if your sins have been legion—send you to a specialist for really sophisticated punishments.

Screening programs could be called a Comedy of Errors if the results weren't so often less than funny. The tuberculin test, for example, was originally very valuable as a method of identifying people who required further investigation for tuberculosis. But the current very low incidence of tuberculosis means that the test has instead become used as a method of "preventive management." This means that in order to prevent the possible one case out of 10,000 or more, potent and dangerous drugs such as INH are given for months and months to people who are so-called "primary reactors." There is also considerable psychological damage that can result when a person becomes a social pariah because friends and neighbors find out that he or she is a positive reactor. Doctors now have to caution mothers against letting neighbors and even relatives know that a child has had a positive tuberculin test, since the test doesn't usually indicate communicability in a child.

If you follow the sounds of medical-governmental drum-beating in favor of a "preventive" procedure, you'll more often than not find yourself in the midst of one of the Church's least safe and effective sacraments. For instance, with some immunizations the danger in *taking* the shot may outweigh that of not taking it!

Diphtheria, once an important cause of disease and death, has all but disappeared. Yet immunizations continue. Even when a rare outbreak of diphtheria does occur, the immunization can be of questionable value. During a 1969 outbreak of diphtheria in Chicago, four of the sixteen victims had been "fully immunized against the disease," according to the Chicago Board of Health. Five others had received one or more doses of the vaccine, and two of these people had tested at full immunity. In another report of diphtheria cases, three of which were fatal, one person who died and fourteen out of twenty-three carriers had been fully immunized.

The effectiveness of the whooping cough vaccine is hotly debated all over the world. Only about half of its recipients benefit, and the possibility of high fevers, convulsions, and brain damage is too high to ignore. So great are the dangers that many public health authorities now prohibit the use of the vaccine after age six. Meanwhile, whooping cough itself has almost completely disappeared.

Whether or not the mumps vaccine is advisable is also in doubt. While the vaccine definitely lowers the incidence of mumps in those who receive it, it does so at the risk of exposing them to the dangers of mumps later on after the immunity has worn off. Furthermore, diseases such as mumps, measles, and German measles—for which vaccines have been developed over the past few years—don't have the dread implications of smallpox, tetanus, and diphtheria. Contrary to popular belief, measles cannot cause blindness. Photophobia, which is merely a *sensitivity* to light, can be treated as parents years ago did: by pulling down the windowshades. Measles vaccine is supposed to prevent measles encephalitis, which is said to occur in one out of 1,000 cases. Any doctor who has had decades of experience with measles knows that while the incidence may be that high among children who live under poverty and malnutrition, among well-nourished middle and upper class children the incidence is one in 10,000 or even one in 100,000. Meanwhile, the vaccine itself is associated with encephalopathy in one case per million and more frequently with other neurologic and sometimes fatal conditions such as ataxia (discoordination), retardation, hyperactivity, aseptic meningitis, seizures, and hemiparesis (paralysis of one side of the body).

German measles or rubella vaccine remains controversial in that there is little consensus regarding the age at which people should be immunized. Vaccine for rubella may also do more harm than good, since there is a risk of arthritis arising from the drug which, although temporary, may last for months. In the United States, rubella vaccine is given to children rather than to women contemplating pregnancy. It's debatable whether this does any good in protecting unborn fetuses since the rate of deformed babies born to mothers with obvious, diagnosed rubella varies from one year to the next, from one epidemic to the next, and from one study to the next.

Immunization isn't the only factor determining whether or not a person contracts a disease. Numerous other factors such as nutrition, housing, and sanitation all figure strongly. Doubts persist as to whether the whooping cough (pertussis) vaccine has really had much to do with the decline in that disease—as well as to whether the vaccine would pass Food and Drug Administration standards if introduced today.

Sometimes the vaccine itself can trigger the disease. In September, 1977, Jonas Salk testified along with some other scientists that of a handful of polio cases which had occurred in the United States since the early 1970s most were likely the byproduct of the live polio vaccine which is in standard use here. In Finland and Sweden, where the killed virus is used almost exclusively, there have been no cases of polio in ten years. No one who lived through the 1940s and saw children in iron lungs, saw a president confined to his wheelchair, or who was forbidden from using public beaches for fear of catching polio, can forget the frightening spectre raised in our minds. Today, when the man credited with stamping out polio points to the vaccine as the source of the handful of cases which do exist, it's high time to question what we are gaining by using the vaccine on an entire population.

The mad vehemence of Modern Medicine is nowhere more evident than in the yearly influenza vaccine farce. I can never think about flu shots without remembering a wedding I once attended. Strangely enough, no grandparents were among the participants and no one seemed to be over age 60. When I finally asked where all the old folks were, I was told they had all received their flu shots a few days before. They were all at home recovering from the shots' ill effects!

The entire flu shot effort resembles some massive roulette game, since from one year to the next it's anybody's guess whether the strains immunized against will be the strains that are epidemic. We were all afforded a peek at the real dangers of flu vaccines when in 1976, the Great Swine Flu Fiasco revealed, under close government and media surveillance, 565 cases of Guillain-Barre paralysis resulting from the vaccine and thirty "unexplained" deaths of older persons within hours after receiving the shot. I wonder what would be the harvest of disaster if we kept as close a watch on the effects of all the other flu shot campaigns. Dr. John Seal, of the National Institute of Allergy and Infectious Disease, says, "We have to go on the basis that any and all flu vaccines are capable of causing Guillain-Barre syndrome."

Again, besides children and old people, women are more vulnerable and, therefore, more often abused by the medical profession. No good evidence exists that screening for breast cancer does anybody any good. Yet doctors have whipped the populace into such a frenzy over breast cancer "prevention" that what I can only call "Alice-in-Wonderlandish" events start to occur. Consider the suggestion that the danger of breast cancer and other female-associated cancers is so great in some families that surgical removal of breasts and ovaries should be performed as a preventive measure! Another example of this sort of "preventive surgery" is the current practice of vaginectomy (removal of the vagina) in adult women who have no symptoms but whose mothers received DES during their pregnancies. Women should be very careful what they tell their doctors about themselves or their family. You never know what he might want to remove from your body in order to "protect" you! Men, on the other hand, probably don't have to be so careful, since doctors will never start surgically removing penises to protect men from anything.

Of course, besides the fact that these "preventive measures" are ineffective and harmful, doctors do further harm by withholding information that might *really* prevent disease. I'm thinking of the four causes of breast cancer which all women *should* know about. I'd be willing to wager that very few of the women who do know these four causes found out about them from their doctor. The four ingredients in the recipe for breast cancer are: small number of children or no children at all, bottle-feeding rather than breastfeeding, use of the Pill, and use of post-menopausal hormones such as Premarin.

Another campaign carried on against women in the name of "prevention" is the widely promulgated notion that women over thirty shouldn't have children. When I was in medical school, I was taught that women should not have babies if they're older than forty-five. By the time I was an intern, it was down to forty. When I was a resident, thirty-eight. Ten years ago it was down to thirty-five. And now it's hovering between thirty and thirty-two. The reason usually given by doctors for restrictions on the age of a mother is that something happens to the eggs of a woman as she gets older, they get worn out and tired. So we have *"tired egg"* syndrome causing deformities in babies. You never hear anything about "tired" *sperms.*

Actually, age has nothing to do with whether a mother gives birth to a deformed baby. A study at Johns Hopkins revealed that the incidence of dental and medical *x-rays* in mothers who have given birth to Mongoloid children is seven times as high as in mothers of comparable age who have given birth to normal children. This study has been backed up by other studies, too, so the *real* cause of deformed babies is associated with age only in that older women—if they haven't been careful—have exposed themselves to more medical, dental, therapeutic, and largely useless x-rays.

At the other end of life, women are told not to have babies if they're too *young!* Teenage pregnancies have a bad reputation, but again, the real threat has nothing to do with the age of the mother. Teenage pregnancies get their bad reputation from the fact that most of them occur in poor women. If a middle or upper class, well-nourished and cared for teenager gets pregnant, she has as good a chance—maybe better—as anyone of having a healthy baby.

Modern Medicine's brand of preventive medicine is so dangerous that we really should abandon the term. There's nothing wrong with the idea that people should take care of themselves so that they won't get sick, but Modern Medicine's concept of prevention is as far from that as you can get. Preventive medicine performed by the Church is as oppressive and dangerous as "curative" medicine—maybe more so, since doctors *use* the shield of preventive medicine to hide any number of truly *aggressive* procedures.

In the first place, Modern Medicine does not address itself to health. Most doctors don't know how to describe a healthy person. The most they can come up with is, "This is normal." Furthermore, since the doctor can run the patient through an incredible arsenal of tests, the limits of what is "normal" are practically all-exclusive. There's always going to be *something* wrong with you, because the doctor doesn't get anything out of the situation if you're "normal," or healthy.

Public health doctors were once held by their colleagues in very low esteem. They dealt with sanitation and other basic items that tended to keep people *away* from doctors. However, since public health doctors have adopted *screening* as their primary activity, they're now held in very high esteem because they are the *procurers* of Modern Medicine. They *deliver* patients instead of keep them away.

Modern Medicine doesn't believe that a person *can* do anything about staying healthy, since doctors believe that disease is just a curse inflicted anonymously and warded off not by concrete actions but by symbolic sacraments that bear no relation to the real world.

And because Modern Medicine recognizes no sins but those against its laws, everyone comes into the world with the original sin of potential disease. Doctors *assume* you're sick until you prove otherwise. You cannot be cleansed merely by "claiming" to be healthy and symptom-free. You have to go through the exam, the proof of your immunizations, and the "confession" of your and your family's history. Doctors make judgments just like other priests. When you are questioned during the "confession," and asked whether you've ever had venereal disease, do you know what the doctor writes down if you say you've never had VD? He writes: "Patient *denies* VD." There are no other diseases that doctors are taught to write "patient *denies*."

If a doctor practices *real* preventive medicine, his patients are going to be healthier and will therefore require fewer visits to his office. You can see right away that this is as contrary as you can get to Modern Medicine's idea. The Church is primarily interested in its authority, so anything that lessens it—such as fewer visits to the doctor—is taboo. Modern Medicine thrives on disease, not health. The more frightened people become of all the disease "out there" waiting to strike them down *randomly,* the more susceptible they are to the come-ons and put-downs of Modern Medicine.

One of the mechanisms doctors use to enhance the general frenzy is the Blame The Victim game. It's *your fault* if you're sick, *not* because of disease-producing habits you developed and refused to exchange for health-producing ones, but because you didn't receive the sacraments of Modern Medicine soon enough or at all. Though a doctor will never give up and declare a patient "in God's hands" until he has exhausted his supply of potions, mutilations, and sacrifices, a patient sometimes goes all the way to God sooner than expected. Even when the worst occurs, doctors never admit that it was the sacrament that killed. Using their semantic privilege they turn it around and make it the victim's fault. *He was too far gone.*

If you believe in Modern Medicine, you believe that you never really can *expect* health. You never really know what to expect, since disease is a random process. You live in a neurotic state of tension, fear, and guilt, anesthetized against your responsibilities and powers. You are primed to be passively taken over by the nearest will stronger than your own.

The fact that patients often don't take their medicine drives doctors up the wall. Patient compliance is a very big research field, because Modern Medicine wants to improve its methods of getting patients to do what it tells them. The ideal would be a constant electronic monitoring system that would allow the doctor to keep tabs on the "compliance" of every patient, with perhaps an optional electronic buzzer or "cattle" prod to remind the patient to take his medicine. Until this kind of enforcement of doctor's orders becomes socially acceptable, Modern Medicine has to satisfy itself with keeping the flock in line through more conventional, indeed *medieval,* methods.

When enough people are radicalized by too good a look at a religion, that religion goes on the defensive and institutes a *theology.* To prevent heretics from unsettling a comfortable status quo, church fathers *freeze* the religion's beliefs and practices and invent or exaggerate the importance of already existing mythology. By harking back to previous successes, the doctor-priest glorifies contemporary practices by giving them the aura of divine revelation. Then, to protect the priest's interpretation of the divine, Modern Medicine declares itself infallible.

Argue with that and you're a heretic. Anything outside the narrow sight of Church Law, any treatment not part of standard procedure, is termed unorthodox, thereby banishing it to a netherworld of suspicion*.

I've already discussed how Modern Medicine neutralizes effective preventive action by ignoring true causes of disease. The same

*Modern Medicine has grown so corrupt that not only does its Vision fail to inspire faith and devotion, but its sacraments and symbols cannot move people to a better life. So Modern Medicine has started to become *more than defensive.* It must rely on *force* to maintain itself and grow. As its spiritual authority has diminished, Modern Medicine has grown more oppressive and violent. What was once the option of a free people is becoming an enforced obligation.

We have a Medical Inquisition.

The first, seemingly innocuous, sign of an inquisition is the selling of indulgences. By promoting the selling of indulgences, a church admits that it has lost any rightful claim on people's imaginations and hearts. When you can *buy* your blessings, a religion motivates you not to good works but to whatever will allow you to purchase your place in "heaven."

mechanism by which we are taught that heart disease is a matter of chance rather than diet and lifestyle is also used to divert our gaze from other causes of disease, namely, *political* causes.

Most of the diseases which are killing us nowadays are the result of "pollution" of our physical, political, economic, community, family, and individual psychological environments. True preventive medicine cannot ignore these issues when addressing a problem of health, yet doctors declare the problems strictly medical, thus solvable through the sacraments of the Church of Modern Medicine.

One of my favorite examples of this process is lead poisoning. Doctors are taught in medical school that the cause of lead poisoning is *pica*. Pica is defined as any abnormal appetite for non-food substances. In this case, the offending substance is lead. Where do the children get the lead? From windowsills and various parts of a building where paint is peeling. As long as we believe that, we don't recognize the root cause of lead poisoning, which is that *the child is eating paint off the windowsills because there's no food in the refrigerator.* Even in the days of interior lead-based paint, middle and upper class children never got lead poisoning. Why should they eat paint? They can go to the refrigerator when they're hungry!

If we are allowed to see the real cause of lead poisoning as hunger, we either must write off the children in danger or decide to address the problem at its roots, since the medical treatment of lead poisoning is mostly ineffective and often dangerous. Once you decide to get at the roots of the problem of lead poisoning, you open a closet full of medical-political skeletons. After you look at hunger, you have to look at lead in the air from fuel burning, lead in toothpaste,

The Church of Modern Medicine passed that point long ago. Medical insurance is the doctor's version of indulgences. Whereas most traditional religions never demanded more than ten percent, the Church of Modern Medicine's price tag on its blessings and sacraments increases faster than anything else in the marketplace. You buy *future blessings* because Modern Medicine tacitly admits it can't maintain your health, so you're going to need these blessings someday. This lets the doctor off the hook and puts you on it. The doctor can't lose and you can't win, because you're tricked into believing that you're going to get sick no matter what you do. What a way to go through life! What a spiritual inspiration!

Besides, medical insurance has accomplished little in terms of protecting the patient. After all, considering the deductibles, a hospitalized patient today is likely to spend just as much money as a few decades ago before insurance. The almost exclusive effect of medical

and lead in baby formula. It's so much simpler to blame the mother for letting the child suck on paint. Of course, it also makes the political climate much more amenable to the growth of Modern Medicine.

Medical sanction and promotion of birth control at all costs and small families doesn't serve any proven medical purpose, but it sure serves the interests of the industry-government complex. Once again, women and children are on the wrong end of the process. Many women *must* work in an outside job merely to make ends meet in the household. That strikes me as a political-economic problem more than anything else, since the head of a household—man or woman—should be able to support the family without the other adult having to go to work. Facing *that* problem requires taking on some of the basic inequities of our society. So we call in the doctors to medicalize the situation. Since large families require a mother (or father) to stay around the house longer before going to seek employment, doctors declare small families better than large ones. Then, doctors supply the apparatus needed to keep families small and put less strain on the institutions that like to maintain economic and political control, institutions that would have to yield some power if it suddenly became an issue that one wage-earner per family was simply not enough anymore.

Large families require more *time* and *money,* but they also provide a *support* for their members, which ultimately makes them more independent of the government and the industrial employer. If a man has brothers, sisters, aunts, uncles, and parents close-by, he can count on their support if conditions on the job make working more unhealthy than not working. But when the family is small and iso-

insurance has been to enhance the income of the providers.

Like the medieval Inquisition, the Medical Inquisition assumes you're guilty. External acts of health will not sway your doctor. The fact that you can run marathon distances will only make your doctor suspicious of you, and won't convince him that you're healthy. He's more likely to warn you against hurting yourself. Also like the medieval Inquisition, all your business with the Church is secret—even from you. Try getting copies of your medical records.

The medieval Inquisition was not accountable for its actions. Neither is the Medical Inquisition. If the medieval Inquisition executed or tortured a witness to death, no matter. There was probably something sinful about him anyway. If in the course of your treatment your doctor kills you because of stupidity, negligence, or just plain malevolence, your family will need the best lawyer money can buy to have a chance of getting justice. If your

lated from relatives, there is no such cushion at home. The nuclear family best serves the interests of the employer, since the worker has enough responsibility to require employment, but not enough to motivate him to exceed the limits acceptable to industry. When the *home* is strong, however, job, hospital, and government have less chance of appropriating the will of the people. Doctors promise a woman "liberation" from her biology, but deliver her into the hands of far less considerate slavers. Doctors don't really address the problem of what causes cancer. They declare a "War on Cancer" which is a futile assault on symptoms. Identifying the pollution of our air, water, food, and lifestyle would require the same kind of political action Modern Medicine mustered to elevate immunizations, fluoridation, and silver nitrate to the level of Holy Waters enforced by law.

Because Modern Medicine is the Church of Death, the stronger its influence on society, the worse off all human elements will be. A public order brought about through the tools of Modern Medicine will resemble the peace of the cemetery. Wherever Modern Medicine gains significant influence in the life of a community, that community is more often than not harmed rather than helped. Government food programs dictated by nutritional experts, for example, assault minority communities by forcing them to eat "standardized" American food, which may be intolerable to their habits as well as their biology. In school lunch programs and nutrition programs for older people, little attention is paid to cultural, familial, or religious food traditions. Modern Medicine simply says that everybody needs the Big Four: vegetables and fruits, grains, meats, and dairy products. We know, of course, that many cultures cannot tolerate cow's milk because of enzymatic deficiencies. We also know that

doctor kills you because the recognized sacred treatment he uses on you is bogus though no one will admit it, then the best lawyer in the world won't be able to get justice. This happens thousands of times each day.

Most people have some idea of the dictionary definition of the Inquisition: the detection and punishment of heretics. What isn't obvious in the definition is that the Inquisition was actually a very effective tool for enforcing Church law and maintaining the Church as a cultural and political force. The effect was to keep the Church a potent force in people's lives and the life of the culture. You just couldn't get from one end of life or society to the other without paying your dues to the Church.

Try getting from one end of life to the other without paying your dues to Modern Medicine. No one passes through without being dipped or splashed with the already men-

traditional cultural diets are quite nutritious, since they have developed over hundreds of years of adaptation. American nutritional habits, however, are dictated by a variety of considerations, some of which are healthy, but most of which are not.

Communities also are damaged by mass screening programs designed to isolate carriers of certain racially-associated diseases. Screening for Tay-Sachs disease has been controversial within the Jewish community because of its effects on the morale and behavior of anyone who is identified as a carrier. The same is true within the black community, which must endure the invasion of community health officers screening for sickle cell anemia.

The first ingredient in my recipe for turning a healthy community into a slum is to build a hospital right in the middle of it. Once the hospital has established a beachhead, Modern Medicine can launch its first attack, which is against the family. If I were out to destroy family ties among the poor, the first thing I would do is hospitalize them for childbirth and make sure they gave their children formula instead of breastmilk. At the University of Illinois Hospital about thirty years ago, ninety-nine percent of the new mothers were breastfeeding. Today it's down to one percent.

Next, I would institute family planning in poor neighborhoods. I'd hire a whole bunch of poor people to teach contraception to other poor people. The federal government started to do all this twenty-five years ago with the intentions of preventing illegitimacy and venereal disease. What has been the result after twenty-five years? The poor people have more illegitimacy and venereal disease than ever before, and family ties are weaker.

The next thing I want to do, once I've softened them up with

tioned four Holy Waters of Modern Medicine: immunizations, fluoridated water, intravenous fluids, and silver nitrate. All four of these substances are of questionable safety and value—objectively speaking. Nevertheless, Modern Medicine has elevated them to the sacred. To the faithful, not only do these substances carry great power, but it is "taboo" to question or tamper with them. They are to be treated only with reverence, and they are *maintained* in their holiness by *civil law* as well as the Church of Medicine's law.

An Inquisition makes it easier for a church to discredit and disenfranchise competing churches, simply by declaring the competition's rituals to be heresy. Any group of people, ideas, or practices that can affect health is attacked, including traditional religions and the family.

The Inquisition gives Modern Medicine the power it needs to prosecute the competition

forays of infant formula and family planning, is to make the inhabitants of poor neighborhoods—black people—feel inferior. So I institute a sickle cell anemia screening program which identifies one out of seven blacks as carriers. Then I reassure the carriers just as I reassure people with functional heart murmurs, that it doesn't mean anything to be a carrier. Of course, they don't believe it for a minute. They are convinced they've got "bad blood," so they have to be careful about whom they marry, and they let it weigh them down for the rest of their lives.

So much for the poor neighborhoods.

Doctors make sure other segments of society remain poor, too. Discrimination against old people begins with the "curse" on them, which says they will necessarily decline in all talents and abilities which make people worthwhile members of society. Thus medically cursed, the old person is forced to retire and become a ward of the state, or—better still—a ward of the Church as an inmate of a rest home.

Of course, the ultimate goal is that we would *all* become wards of Modern Medicine. Doctors exhibit a dangerous tendency to take advantage of every opportunity to *force* individuals to do things just for the sake of doing them. If doctors didn't want more and more power over the individual, why would more and more medical procedures be showing up as laws? Why should you have to fight with a doctor in order to have your baby at home, breastfeed it, send it to school, or treat its illnesses in any manner you believe effective?

with the force of law behind it. If a doctor "suspects" a child had been the victim of child abuse, the state has given the doctor the power to incarcerate the child in the hospital. What is there to prevent the doctor from suspecting child abuse in any number of situations where the doctor's power is threatened? A lot of people are currently getting around the immunization laws by forging the records or by taking advantage of slack enforcement by school officials. What would happen if both sides got tough at the same time, if the parents publically refused to *submit* and the school refused to *admit?* What's to stop the doctors from accusing the parents of child abuse and taking the children away from them, or, at least, fining them punitively?

In return for the power granted the Inquisition by the state, Modern Medicine does an enormous favor for the state by medicalizing problems that are not medical at all. As John McKnight, Professor of Communications Studies and Associate Director of the Center for Urban Affairs at Northwestern University, has said in his essay "The Medicalization of

I'm not too surprised that normally alert and powerful organizations like the labor unions and the American Civil Liberties Union haven't responded to this threat against our freedom. They fail to acknowledge the problem because they subscribe to the religion of Modern Medicine. Instead of saying that every person is entitled to *not* have an x-ray or an abortion, they say the opposite. They won't notice when the Church requires first older mothers, then all mothers, to submit to amniocentesis to rule out birth defects. They won't notice when the Church forces these mothers to have abortions, either. And when your turn before the Medical Authorities comes up—who knows what for? Maybe you'll need preventive surgery—you'll stand alone.

Whenever a revolutionary group adopts a word, the reactionary group coopts it. This is precisely what Modern Medicine has done with the term "preventive medicine." By making a distinction between preventive medicine and other forms of medicine, the Church controls the concept and *legitimizes* its own obsession with crisis medicine.

If they want to call what they're doing preventive medicine, let them. But let's not call anything *we* do preventive medicine. On the other hand, if they want to label revolutionary procedures according to their own interests, that's OK, too. You can be referred to as child abuser for encouraging mothers to have their babies at home. If necessary, instead of fighting over the words, you should be perfectly willing to be identified as a child abuser. If somebody says

Politics," "The essential function of medicine is the medicalization of politics through the propagation of therapeutic ideology. This ideology, stripped of its mystifying symbols, is a simple triadic credo:

1. The basic problem is you.
2. The resolution of your problem is my professional control.
3. My control is your help.

"The essence of the ideology is its capacity to hide control behind the magic cloak of therapeutic help. Thus, medicine is the paradigm for modernized domination. Indeed, its cultural hegemony is so potent that the very meaning of politics is being redefined. Politics is (usually) interactive—the debate of citizens regarding purpose, value, and power. Medicalized politics is unilateral—the decision of the 'helpers' in behalf of the helped."

that breastfeeding ties down mothers and increases the child's dependency, say you're in favor of mothers being tied down and of children being dependent on their mothers. If anybody says that people who want their food to be pure and natural are nuts, faddists, and extremists, refer to yourself and your friends as nuts, faddists, and extremists. Modern Medicine may label unorthodox doctors as quacks; maybe what we need is more "quacks." Words aren't important. Action is. And the kind of action that's required is nothing less than the destruction of the Church of Modern Medicine.

Across the country there are hundreds of brilliant people performing research on ways to fight and prevent killer diseases such as cancer and heart disease, but because their ways aren't orthodox, they must tread on very light feet if they don't want to be hounded out of town by the Church. Witness the denial of funds to Nobel Laureate Linus Pauling, who simply wanted the National Cancer Institute to grant a modicum of funds to find out if ascorbic acid really provided some benefit for cancer patients—which his earlier research indicated. Witness the fact that more than one doctor I have spoken to has admitted that he would use outlawed cancer therapies on himself or his family. Is this the kind of system you can work within?

People should work to liberate themselves completely from Modern Medicine. It will take an army of heretics with firm resolve to be free of Modern Medicine and with the courage, cunning, and resources to reconstruct society's attitudes towards health and disease.

What's needed is a New Medicine, a new vision of medical care.

9
The New Medicine

The New Medicine is my recipe for winning, my blueprint for the defeat of the Church of Modern Medicine.

Up to now I've been telling you why and how you should protect yourself from Modern Medicine. I've told you how to deceive the doctor, how to find out if his advice is good, how to check up on him, how to scare him, how to confront him, and how to maintain your health despite his dangerous practices.

Maybe you've tried some of these recommendations, or maybe you're just reading this book for entertainment. If you have tried any of them, you're probably aware that you've been doing somewhat more than protecting yourself. You've been *subverting* Modern Medicine. I've told you to lie to your doctor, to shuffle and smile—and to organize behind his back with people who think the way you do about health. I've told you to leave the Church of Modern Medicine and not to challenge it and become a martyr.

I've been setting you up.

One of my favorite mottoes is that there comes a time to rise above principle and to do what has to be done. Once you put any part of my recipe into practice, you'll find out pretty quickly that deciding to protect yourself from your doctor inevitably leads to a much more profound commitment. A single first step towards the New Medicine will render you unable to stand still. You'll either have to retreat and let the doctors run your life again, or you'll have to keep going forward. Maybe you'll start by deciding you want to have your baby at home, or that you want to breastfeed your baby, or that you want to enroll your children in school without immunizing them, or that you want to skip this year's annual job physical, or that you want to pin down your doctor on why he recommends surgery, or that you want the doctor to do something for you or your child without using drugs.

Commit yourself to any one of these things and my guess is that your experience will be the first chink in the glass, the radicalizing experience that will lead to your becoming a medical guerrilla. I'm giving you fair warning.

On the other hand, you don't have to take a loyalty oath to join this revolution. We don't need symbolic protestations of devotion with more symbolic than actual worth. The *practice* of the New Medicine immediately establishes you as loyal.

Taking on the responsibility for your own health and the health of your family constitutes a political act as long as Modern Medicine uses political power to execute its attack on the individual's and the family's right to self-determine health. Our very act of commitment to the *family* as the unit of health and to the community as a collection of families is political because it resists the notion that the *individual* is the unit of health as well as of society.

Our New Medicine cuts across all political and ideological lines and touches the core of every person's relationship with life: *How long and how well will I live?* The New Medicine, too, takes on some of the trappings of a religion.

The Old Medicine became a church because it inevitably dealt with the same problems of life and death and meaning that religions do. It has done a bad job of dealing with them, particularly because it developed a theology based on non-living things. It became a corrupt, idolatrous church. It discredited the old religions, which—for better or for worse—had helped people deal with life and death and everything in between. That is a mistake the New Medicine won't make.

In this book, I have tried my best to discredit the Church of Modern Medicine. Now I can't do that without suggesting an alternative to Modern Medicine. I want to evict the villains from the structure and fill the structure with new people, performing new tasks.

Faith is the first requirement for a religion, and you still need faith to practice the New Medicine. But you won't need faith in technology, or doctors, or drugs, or professionals.

You need faith in life.

By faithfully, *religiously* if you will, regarding life—and loving it—the New Medicine immediately will discredit Modern Medicine. The New Medicine need not come between a person and whatever traditional religion he or she chooses, because the religions that have survived all support life.

Every person needs a system of values, an ethical structure to assist in fundamental decisions. A person who claims to get along without making value judgments is still abiding by a system—of making no value judgments. There's no way to escape it, and that's what religion is all about. Religion defines a hierarchy of values and gives a prescription for action so that people can determine which way to go when alternatives are set before them.

Modern Medicine came along and took over the show by saying, "You no longer have to worry about the values of these other ethical systems, because we can fix anything that happens to you. We release you from the ethics of considering value and, in return, demand only faith in a symbolic ethic, a sacramental ethic, the ethic of our own distorted logic."

No system of logic, distorted or otherwise, ever got around biology. And in biology, the New Medicine finds its ethic, its value system.

Since life is the central mystery of our New Medicine, our "sacraments" acknowledge and celebrate the life of the universe. The "sins" of the New Medicine, in many cases, turn out to be the virtues of the Church of Modern Medicine: any practice that promotes or condones violence against life. The New Medicine says it's a "sin" to restrict weight gain during pregnancy, to use the Pill freely on the theory that it's safer than pregnancy, to submit to routine annual physicals, to put silver nitrate in babies' eyes, to immunize children routinely, to be ignorant of nutrition, and a host of other activities that Modern Medicine promotes as "healthy." These activities are sins not because they offend anybody's idea of correct or polite behavior, but because they present a clear and present danger to life. They are offenses against biology. Since the life in our bodies seems to have an incredible capacity to *heal itself,* if given the proper conditions the corrective activities of the New Medicine—guilt and penance—will aim at producing those proper conditions. Imbalance is often as difficult to avoid in human life as balance is desirable. Since this is a human medicine, not one bound to the deathly formality of machines, hope is one thing that is never taken away from even the worst "sinner."

The New Medicine doesn't have any empty rituals. You fulfill the "commandments" and celebrate the sacraments by doing *real* things. Naturally, we have priests in this religion, too. But the New Doctor is not the prime mediator between the faithful and the object of faith. The authority of the doctor is severely limited by the individual taking the responsibility upon himself. Still, a system of ethics needs a mediator, a supporter of the faithful in their quest, a *lifeguard* when the quest runs into trouble.

Never forget that the New Doctor's goal is to work himself or herself right out of business, so your dependence on the professional should diminish every day. You have to learn to get along without doctors, because doctors aren't the Oracles of faith. The Oracles of faith, the true celebrants of the religion of life are the *self,* the *family,* and the *community.* From these vessels flow the determinants of health: life, love, and courage.

Your first responsibility is to take care of your body and mind. Food is very important, but not food merely in the sense of bread, water, protein, fiber, and vitamins. You must try to eat pure food and drink pure water. You must find out all you can about which foods are best for you, since what goes into your mouth does make a difference in what comes out. We have other appetites that must be nourished, too. In a sense, everything that comes into your life and body is food. Whether it's nourishing or whether it's junk food is the individual's responsibility, and will determine the self's success in reaching the goal of health. If you spend a lot of time in front of the television, lost in a make-believe world that runs a poor second to real life, you're *wasting the time of your life*, time that should be used to nourish your self and those around you. *Choose your food*. Try to taste and see and hear and smell and touch things that will *add* to your supply of life.

Our New Medicine consecrates *activities* as well as food. Quite simply, there are things people should be doing and shouldn't be doing for themselves, for the sake of their own biological truths, for their own lives. The consecration of food governs what comes into the body. The consecration of activity governs what the individual does with the body and the mind, the muscles and the spirit. All religions have some form of vocation, but the calling from God is usually reserved for those who are going to enter the religion's priesthood. Our New Medicine says that everyone should choose his or her career as if called by God, because in a very real way, everyone does have a vocation: *Everyone is called to live a long and happy life.*

Our New Medicine also requires people to gather together at significant moments of life, such as births, marriages, illnesses, anniversaries, and deaths. Since industrial employment is often geared for production, not for personal health, taking enough time to perform these obligations the way they should be performed may create a dilemma. You may wind up self-employed, or unemployed.

The New Medicine calls for a more balanced approach to career. Build a life around personal goals and humanly satisfying activities. *Life* comes first, not the carrot-on-a-stick promises of the rat race. Organize your time and pursue a career in such a way as to allow participation in life events of significance and beauty.

The *home* is the Temple of our New Medicine, because the home is the individual's fortress against the unhealthy institutions such as industry and the Church of Modern Medicine. If an individual, for example, has to quit his or her job because it becomes a threat to health, the family is there to offer support until a new source of income can be set up. This may sound strange to those of us who have bought the industrial society's notion of the family as a *liability* rather than an *asset*. Industry's purposes are better served if the family is kept small, limited to two children and one or two adults, not if the family is considered in its true sense, the collection of related people of all ages living in close proximity and experiencing important life events *together*. When the family bands together for purposes of defense as well as celebration, no institution can disrupt the lives of its members.

Our New Medicine's regard for the family begins when the family itself begins. Our first "commandment" is "Thou shalt not pay any attention to scales during pregnancy." Instead, you pay attention to the quality of the food you eat, eat the purest and most nourishing food you can get, and stop taking *all* medications. You don't take pills "only when necessary," because there are few doctors who don't believe that pills are *always* "necessary." Same goes for x-rays.

Since our New Medicine is a medicine devoted to life, since birth is the principal event of life, and since the home is the temple of our New Medicine, the birth of the baby ideally occurs at home, away from all the dangers of the hospital and close to all the love and support of the family. The birth of a new family member is an event that should not be isolated from the majority of the family. As soon as possible after the birth, every family member should be there to greet the new arrival and to celebrate. That is how the sacrament of birth is performed, by *celebrating*, complete with a family feast and singing and laughter.

To anyone who's read this book so far, it goes without saying that the new mother breastfeeds her baby *exclusively* at first, say the first six months, and then begins to supplement her milk with solid food prepared from the family's table, not the machines of a food manufacturer.

The usual advice given by doctors is that in raising children parents should be consistent. I believe that the only thing parents should do consistently is love their children and each other. Otherwise, there is no particular virtue in consistency. Parents have a hard enough time without trying to keep track of all that they've done for and said to their children. The family is a living thing and should not be pressed into the conformity of thought and action characteristic of a machine.

I once stated on the radio that when it comes to caring for children, one grandmother is worth two pediatricians. My department chairman phoned me shortly thereafter and announced his intent to replace me with two grandmothers. In every aspect of child care, experts should be regarded with utmost suspicion. Each family must consider the patterns that have proved successful in their family, their culture, their social class, and religion. Experts' opinions should be considered worthless until proved otherwise by the strongest possible evidence. Unfortunately, in order to reach back through the disruption of the family in modern times, it may be necessary to go back to grandparents or even great-grandparents in order to *find out* what these traditional practices were. When the historically validated cultural patterns have been lost, it may be necessary to resort to friends and neighbors who come from healthy traditional backgrounds.

From birth onward, significant events in the life of the family are celebrated *en masse* by the family. We discard the terms "nuclear family" and "extended family," because we're not talking about family if we're not talking about the entire assemblage of blood relatives. *All* generations participate in family life, and relevancy is denied no one because of age. Every family member knows that when the family needs him or her, the family comes first. When a family member has to be hospitalized, there's always a crew of relatives available to ride shotgun.

Death is another one of those unavoidable life experiences that brings the family together. Just as births, birthdays, marriages, and other family events take precedence over career and other activities, the death of a family member requires attendance. No family member dies alone or with only the staff of the intensive care ward to note his or her passing. Life should end where it begins, in the home.

Outside of the home, the "medical guerrilla" doesn't just mind his or her own business, either. The ethic of Modern Medicine, and to a great extent the American ethic, says that the individual should keep to himself. I've already talked about the various ways in which the professional services of doctors and others destroy not only family ties but community ties as well. Our New Medicine, however, says we need those community ties. You are your brother's—and sister's—keeper.

Our New Medicine needs community for a number of interesting reasons. First of all, though the New Medicine is directed at freeing the individual from the disabling and dangerous tendencies of Modern Medicine, we recognize that it's very difficult to sustain this sort of rebellion by yourself. We all need friends, but even more so when we're carrying on a battle against the Medical Inquisition.

Our community is a collection of families relating to one another *as families*. Now this may seem remarkably "old fashioned," but remember, the family is the unit of health, the individual's primary resource. The community can also be a resource for health, but communities are more easily dispersed, and because of the nature of American life, are more often dispersed. This is not to say that people do not and should not draw upon the resources of friends at the far corners of the globe. On the contrary, the community should grow and spread its wings.

Think of a community as a *congregation* of people sharing the same faith. Our community or congregation does not conflict with a family's *religious* congregation, just as our medical "religion" doesn't compete with an individual's religious beliefs.

Of course, you may not be able to find a congregation. In that case, you should start your own. You may be able to start with your own family, or you may have to start with friends, or you may have to *move*. I often tell women who come to me and say they'd like to breastfeed their babies but are not sure they'll be able, to move next door to a woman who has successfully breastfed a number of babies. The important thing is to get close to people who share your ethics and standards. Each of us has only a finite amount of time and energy, and since your major supports and encouragements are going to come from people who think and feel the way you do, you shouldn't feel guilty about growing apart from people who *don't* think and feel the same way.

At the same time, our New Medicine doesn't provide a license for narrowing the scope of your vision to the point where your physical and intellectual life become a matter of routine. You should keep informed of the ethical systems of other religions and ways of health. Don't just read one or two or three books and pronounce yourself saved. Read 100 books! Read every book you can find on the subject of health, especially those that expose the dangerous inadequacies of Modern Medicine, and those that are grounded in traditions that have survived for hundreds of years. (See the Bibliography for a good list to start with.) Get used to the idea right away that no single system can or should claim to have an exclusive fix on the dynamics of health.

Since our New Medicine is a biological "religion," the promised rewards are also biological. The primary rewards will be quantitative: low infant mortality and long life expectancy. Spell that out in terms of quality of life and it means that everybody will be healthier. We will have a low incidence of biological and sociological disease. Biologically, there will be a low incidence of infections, allergies, cancer, heart disease, diabetes, and toxic conditions. Sociologically, there will be a low incidence of divorce, suicide, and depression.

With less disease, there will be less need for the doctor-priest. The number of visits to and by the doctor will drop, the number of procedures performed by doctors will drop, and the price tag for medical care will drop. The doctor will be transformed into a family friend and will no longer be considered the "outside technician" whose skills are the object of awe.

Our community will grow, both internally and externally, because of the liberation of the family from being considered a liability to being considered an asset. Internally, our numbers will grow as families grow larger. Externally, we will grow by attracting more and more people who want to be free of Modern Medicine.

Perhaps more important than the measurable rewards are the rewards that can't be expressed in statistics or dollars and cents. Ours is a medicine of hope, not despair; of joy, not sorrow; of love, not fear. All of our "sacraments" are celebrations. We don't note birthdays, marriages, and other milestones by sucking blood or demanding an offering. We ask for a party! When a woman has a baby at home, it's not only to avoid the dangers of the hospital. It's to make possible the joyous sharing of all family members in the truly blessed event. When a woman nurses her baby, she's going to feel joy she could never feel if the baby were sucking on a plastic nipple attached to a bottle!

Our New Medicine offers the perfect antidote to the major disease afflicting American society today: depression. Depression is a slice of death, and our commitment to life and joy denies us that morsel of despair. The recipe for depression is isolation, abandonment, frustration, and alienation. Our sacraments simply don't let those situations develop. It's very difficult to feel afraid, alone, and unloved when you've got somebody's birthday or baby or marriage or new job or ... whatever to celebrate. When we say that our New Medicine is a community of celebrants, we mean it.

Another reward we can promise is that once you have the alternative of participating in our New Medicine, you learn to regard the "other side" without the fear and hatred that are likely when you have no option, when you have to submit to Modern Medicine. Your original sense of frustration and depression is transformed, into amusement, even. Many recent books and movies have very cleverly exposed some of Modern Medicine's more obvious faults. When you're not aware of alternatives to Modern Medicine, these revelations can hit pretty hard. I and some of my students have come close to being thrown out of movie theaters when our laughter has rung out over an audience's gasps at the screen's depiction of Modern Medicine at its slapstick best ... or worst.

Once you get into our New Medicine, once you realize that your health and the health of your family is a happy and hopeful privilege rather than an ominous liability to be entrusted to strangers, you *will* feel freer and happier. A lot of people have come up to me and said that it's very difficult for someone to embrace this "revolution" unless they've been radicalized. Unless Modern Medicine has severely hurt them or someone close to them, people have told me, they won't begin to see the danger in doctors' procedures we all have come to take for granted. They've told me that people need to be scared before they can feel courage.

All of that may be true. This book has, in a way, been my answer to my friends who have said these things to me. I have written this book precisely to scare and to radicalize people *before* they are hurt. Let this book be your radicalizing experience. Remember what I've said the next time you go to the doctor.

Another thing people ask me is how to start. They want to join the revolution but they don't know exactly where to sign up.

You don't have to sign up. You can start the revolution in your own home tonight. Start thinking of your family as a resource instead of a liability. If you're not married, think seriously about finding somebody and getting married. If you're married, the most revolutionary act you can perform tonight is to conceive a child. Then plan on having the baby at home and breastfeeding him or her.

If your parents are alive, call them up and plan a visit over the phone for the next available weekend. Or do the same with another relative.

Decide what your priorities are in life. Would you really *rather* work on an assembly line making sure this part fits into that part than making sure the pieces of a child's life all fit in place? Are the rewards of the rat race really worth selling so much of your time, energy, and emotional commitment that you don't have any left for your family as well as *yourself?* Is your job really getting you anywhere real other than closer to the coronary care ward?

Search for a community. Ask the next mother you see if she is breastfeeding or has breastfed her baby. The next time somebody says something derogatory about children or old people, say something back. When you go to lunch or dinner, start discussing health with people—not with the intention of arguing, but to find people who *agree* with you. As soon as you find these people, get to know them better. Start your community.

People also come up to me and want to know when the revolution will be over, when they will be able to stop thinking of themselves as medical heretics. I have to admit that I don't know the answer.

I do know that you can tell when you're winning: when you influence those closest to you. When your family and friends start to feel and express the joy that comes from knowing that health is a matter of choice, not a mystery of chance. That can happen when you or a relative breastfeeds a baby that's born at home, or when you or a relative decides to double-check a doctor's prescription for surgery and not only avoids the surgery but finds a doctor who helps solve the problem without as much as a hypodermic needle.

A few months ago, I became a grandfather. Our daughter delivered an eight-pound, one-ounce baby girl. Channa was born, as we planned, in our home. In attendance was my daughter's husband, her sister, her mother, Mayer Eisenstein, M.D., and myself. Both labor and delivery followed an almost classic pattern and lasted about five hours from beginning to end. After Channa was born, relatives and friends began to visit. They barely paused to greet me at the door before rushing up to greet Channa. For the five weeks that the new family stayed at our house before moving off to their own new home in Canada, I was able to leave the house every morning while the new mother was asleep and the new grandmother was rocking the new granddaughter on the porch. And on his way home those summer afternoons, the new grandfather didn't have to stop off at the hospital to get a peek at his granddaughter behind glass. I could go right home and gaze at her all through dinner.

So I can tell we're winning.

I can tell we're winning because the people I see already practicing our New Medicine appear to be the healthiest people in our society. The people of the La Leche League and NAPSAC and SPUN and similar organizations not only can turn out thousands and thousands at their meetings, but when they travel from city to city, they use each other as points of reference. *They have a community.*

I can tell we're winning because in the eyes of all these families and in my own family I can see the satisfaction, the optimism, and the joy when human beings know that they are the owners of their own health.

Epilog
In Search of
the New Doctor

Health neither begins nor ends with the doctor. The doctor's role is somewhere in the middle. And still crucial. If doctors weren't important, the Church of Modern Medicine could never have gained the power it has.

This simultaneous process of destroying Medicine and rebuilding Medicine is, by nature, a political process. *At all levels,* the Medical Revolution involves the participant in politics: If you keep your children out of public school to avoid immunizing them, that is a political act. If you have your baby at home when state laws discourage it or health insurance refuses to pay for it, that's a political act. If you decide to have *another baby,* that's a political act. While we turn our backs on the Inquisition, we turn towards and embrace the New Medicine *as we need to in order to survive and prosper.* That is going to require action which is *explicitly* political, too.

As John McKnight has said in his essay, "The Medicalization of Politics," "Politics is the act of citizens pooling their intelligence to achieve the maximum human good. Medicalized politics is the disavowal of that common intelligence. Politics is the art of the possible—a process that recognizes limits and grapples with the questions of equity imposed by those limits. Medicalized politics is the art of the impossible—the process by which an unlimited promise is substituted for justice. Politics is the art of reallocating power. Medicalized politics mystifies control so that power is no longer an issue. The central political issue becomes the right to more control. Politics is *the act of citizens*. Medicalized politics is the *control of clients*. Only the hands of citizens can cure medicine. Medicine cannot cure itself because its prescriptions come from its own system of values."

If your community is considering fluoridating the water—or if it already has fluoridated water—you may have to fight it. You may take political action and work against the enactment of national health insurance, or work for the inclusion of "revolutionary clauses" which will prevent the Inquisition from getting a death grip on our society. You may work politically for laws which will effectively remove poisons from our air, food, and water. Or for changes in the Social Security and tax laws that will favor keeping families together and strong.

I recently was asked by a group of Latin-American mothers in Chicago to help promote breastfeeding among the members of their organization for better child raising. They knew their biggest problem was that the community hospitals these women were using sanctioned the use of formula. The mothers decided to do something with their organization. They visited the heads of the hospitals and tried to persuade them to stop encouraging bottlefeeding by handing out free sixpacks of formula and special "supplementary feeding packs" to mothers who already were breastfeeding. They said that if the hospital heads did not respond to their requests, they were going to picket the hospitals.

It seems to me that the New Doctor has to be in the front lines of these struggles. He or she will have to be involved politically if only in response to his patients' needs. He or she will be visible through the newspapers and other media when these issues come to the fore. And if they *don't* come there, he'll make sure they *do*.

This is one of the major differences between the ethics of Modern

Medicine and those of the New Medicine. Modern Medicine tells doctors to stay out of politics. Of course, this is merely to hide the fact that doctors are already into politics in an immensely powerful way. The Church likes the status quo, since it is in control, so it wants to be able to scare away potential troublemakers and blacken the reputations of those who can't be scared away, by labeling them "politicians."

The New Medicine says that the doctor is not a monastic priest sitting in his monastery, but is a participant in the life of the community. Doctors will be community leaders active in politics because concern for the health of the community demands it. When the water company wants to fluoridate the public water, the New Doctor will be right there to make sure people know the biological consequences. When the power company wants to build a nuclear power plant, the New Doctor will not stand by and let the health of the community be threatened. Rather than allow political issues to become medicalized—and thus defused—the New Doctor will acknowledge the need for political power to be applied to matters of health and disease. He or she will not shrink from identifying "bad" politics as factors in disease.

Community involvement of this nature implies a certain type of doctor with the *sensitivities*, *skills*, and *motivation* to help build the New Medicine. Any collection of ideas-for-action can be subverted by the people who do the acting.

The New Doctor is comfortable with people from all walks of life—not only in the doctor-patient relationship, but in social relationships as well. The New Doctor considers his or her service as an agent of social improvement, so he or she will need to understand and be aware of the social and ethical foundations of medicine.

The New Doctor will be conversant not only in the language of science, but in the language of *people* as well. He or she is going to be constantly *informing* patients: informing them of the risks and benefits of prospective treatments, informing them of the ways they can stay healthy, informing them of how certain activities and circumstances affect health. The doctor-patient relationship is democratic in the sense that both doctor and patient share information equally. But that "democracy" must necessarily break down when the doctor has to exercise his or her authority. The "perfect" example of this is when the patient is unconscious. Obviously, under those circumstances the doctor must accept responsibility and make choices in the best interests of the patient—without the patient's consent. When the patient *is* conscious, however, the doctor must still recognize that there might be a point at which the patient's knowledge ends and the doctor's keeps going. That's why the patient is seeing the doctor, after all, to depend—however much—on that knowledge and training. I don't care whether the doctor wears blue jeans or a three-piece suit, whether his or her hair is short or long, whether he works out of a brand-new clinic or a used van—the patient is there for the benefit of the doctor's knowledge. The doctor must inform the patient of how the patient's choices will affect him, but he or she must not shrink from making a judgment based on his or her knowledge and talents. That's what the patient is paying for.

When the New Doctor is faced with a patient who has just had a baby, that patient is going to be informed of what her alternatives are for feeding and caring for that baby. The New Doctor is going to tell her that bottle feeding is not as safe or healthy as breastfeeding, and that the difference in benefit and risk is great enough so that if she chooses to bottle feed, she is going to have to find another doctor.

The New Doctor is not afraid to act on evidence that's available *today*. He or she has enough confidence in his or her knowledge, training, and instincts to avoid the cop out: "We don't know enough. All the evidence isn't in. We need more research."

Because the New Doctor admits up front that these choices are necessary, he or she must be aware and responsive to the ethics of the doctor-patient relationship. To what extent do people have stewardship over life, death, and health? How far can medicine increase our control over life and death? What issues are involved in the choices to use artificial organs, transplanted organs, and artificial life-extending machinery? It's not enough for the New Doctor to know *how* to do things, but *why*. Just because something *can* be done, does that mean it *should* be done? The ethic that will permeate the New Doctor's practice and training is regard for the rights and dignity of human beings.

As maker of health, the New Doctor is aware that the patient and nature are the ingredients, not merely the medium for the expression of technique. Aware of the limits of human competence, the New Doctor knows when to intervene in natural processes, when to encourage natural processes, and when to let natural processes run their course. Implied in this knowledge is awareness of the harm that can be done by doctors.

"The art of medicine," according to a colleague and good friend of mine, Leo I. Jacobs, M.D., Medical Director of Forest Hospital, Des Plaines, Illinois, "flows from the physician's ability to be introspective and to understand the patient as a human being with certain feelings, thoughts, attitudes, interpersonal relationships, aspirations, and expectations rather than a mere symptom carrier. Such a physician tends to see the patient, and not himself, as the primary person responsible for maintaining health, by leading a meaningful life in which proper nutrition, exercise, and stress management combine with an appropriate balance of love, play, and work within a harmonious family. Such a physician will resort to drugs or surgery only after his understanding of the patient's predicament has ruled out non-invasive or educational, psychological, or social approaches."

The New Doctor acknowledges nature as the prime healer, and so regards natural supports of health, such as the family, as having supreme importance in the healing process. The family is the unit of health and disease, so the New Doctor treats the whole person in the context of family as well as religion and social system. The New Doctor makes house calls and meets the family on its own turf. He or she disregards professional language and advice that tends to split families into warring factions. Proper avoidance of hospitalization will be a key goal, so the New Doctor delivers babies at home and scorns the idea that people must come into and leave this world under conditions of intensive care.

The New Doctor is a *lifeguard*. He or she stands by ready to intervene in life-threatening situations. At the beginning of life he lets the mother deliver the baby and stands by for the tiny percentage of cases in which he is needed.

As soon as we assign the role of lifeguard to the doctor, we define what he does and does not do throughout his career. He or she does not play the central role. The central roles are played by the individual, the family, and the community.

And in "guarding" the health of his patients, the New Doctor establishes priorities according to their promise of safety and effectiveness. The Hippocratic order of treatment placed *regimen* before medicine and surgery. So will the New Doctor. What a patient does every day with and to the body and soul have a greater effect on health than what the doctor can do in a small fraction of that time. The New Doctor must teach the patient what to do during the mass of time he is living his life on his own, away from the doctor, to maintain and maximize health.

The one rule I give to all my medical students is that I don't care what you do to the patient as long as he or she feels better when leaving the office than when coming in. The New Doctor heals with *himself*. If the doctor has enthusiasm and hope, and can communicate this to the patient, then the patient is going to feel better. A healer is a healer no matter what techniques he uses. Conscious of this, the New Doctor prescribes "himself" in generous doses, meaning he or she uses whatever resources of personality and human caring possible.

The New Doctor still will be a priest in the sense that he or she will officiate or mediate at the absolution or cleansing of the patient's "sins." You'll still have to confess to the New Doctor, in the sense that you will give your "history" and the doctor will identify what is health-producing and health-destroying in your life. The New Doctor doesn't presume you're never going to do anything unhealthy, but he's going to make sure you're aware of it when you do. We know that the body has its own powers of absolution in its incredible ability to adapt and make up for "mistakes." You still have to do penance, but there's a difference. The New Doctor doesn't sprinkle you with holy water and pronounce you saved if you take this drug or let him mutilate you. The New Doctor doesn't sacrifice you to any vengeful gods. Your penance is biological, it's the price you have to pay to get back in balance. You have to overcompensate for a while to make up for going too far.

Naturally, the New Doctor tries to motivate people to *avoid* disease, too. I believe guilt is one of the strongest motives for changing one's behavior. The New Doctor, being concerned with *causes* of disease rather than superficial symptoms, is going to ascribe guilt in a more rational and ethical fashion than Modern Medicine. The guilt will be personal, but not exclusively personal, and it will be *relieveable* through *action,* not symbolic rituals. In the case of lead poisoning, the guilt will be ascribed to whoever is responsible for the lack of food in the refrigerator, whoever is responsible for the lead in the air, in infant formula, and in food. If a woman opts for analgesia and anesthesia during childbirth, she deserves some guilt because these things are not good for the baby. If a mother tells the New Doctor she's planning to bottle feed her baby, the New Doctor is going to tell her she's threatening the baby's health. New Doctors will try to make people feel guilty about eating refined sugar and flour and over-processed foods, about smoking, and about not exercising.

The New Doctor's use of guilt will motivate people to healthy habits rather than frustration and fear because there won't be any double-think involved. Something is either good for you or bad for you and the New Doctor will make sure you know the difference. That difference will be determined *biologically* rather than politically or religiously. If bottle feeding is wrong, it's wrong because it exposes mother and baby to a number of unhealthy conditions, such as gastroenteritis, allergies, infections, and inadequate bonding between mother and child. The New Doctor may believe that a woman's body is her own, but *biologically* he or she knows that abortion causes a higher rate of sterility and other complications that a properly informed woman would not choose to expose herself to. A doctor should tell a woman that an abortion will increase the chances of her delivering a premature infant in the future by fifty percent. He should tell her about the Israeli study of more than 11,000 pregnancies in which women who had previous induced abortions "were subsequently less likely to have a normal delivery. In the births following induced abortions, the relative risk of early neonatal death was doubled, while late neonatal deaths showed a three- to four-fold increase. There was a significant increase in the frequency of low birthweight, compared to births in which there was no history of previous abortion. There were increases in major and minor congenital malformations." *(American Journal of Epidemiology,* September, 1975)

The New Doctor's honesty will extend to denying Modern Medicine's mythical claim that everything can be cured, that no matter how you mess yourself up the skills of the doctor can put you back together. The New Doctor informs his or her patients that real cures are hard to come by and that even miracle cures fade fast. Patients are thus cautioned against straying too far away from the balance that will insure them a long and healthy life.

The New Doctor will be skeptical of the promised benefits of drugs and surgery. One of his or her major areas of responsibility is to protect people against the excesses of surgeons and drug companies in foisting off their wares. Nevertheless, the New Doctor does not abandon useful technology, but rather discriminates between useful machinery and machinery for-the-sake-of-machinery. He's trained in the use of scientific equipment, but he's also taught the risks and the deficiencies of it. Most of all, the New Doctor doesn't rely on machinery unless absolutely necessary. He's aware of the dangers of letting technology rule over common sense and instinct.

Since he will reject much of Modern Medicine's machinery, the New Doctor is knowledgeable in unorthodox methods of treating disease, including nutritional therapy, acupuncture, kinesiology, chiropractic, homeopathy, and others.

One of the primary activities of the New Doctor is to protect patients against the excesses of specialists. New Doctors will be antagonists to the specialists: they'll make their patients feel *guilty* about going to a specialist and endangering themselves without justification. Instead of viewing the patient as a collection of symptoms localized in a single spot, the New Doctor will see the whole person as the context and possible cause for disease.

Eventually, in the light of ethics, iatrogenic considerations and exposure, and generalist education of doctors, the specialties will largely disappear. If the hospital addiction can be licked early in life—at birth—it will not become a habit later in life. Home delivery of babies will cause the disappearance of ninety-five percent of obstetrics and gynecology. As the failure of psychiatric chemotherapy, psycho-surgery, electroshock therapy, analysis, and most counseling is exposed—in favor of strong familial, friendship, self-esteem support networks—most of psychiatry will disappear. Internal medicine will go under with its highly lucrative recruiting practices: annual exams, screening for hypertension, and drug therapies for diseases that can be treated naturally. Surgery will mostly disappear as people learn to refuse to let doctors mutilate them for no particularly good reason—and as they are able to find more and more New Doctors who will treat them without surgery. The entire field of orthodox oncology will disappear as chemotherapy, surgery, and radiation for cancer are revealed as fundamentally irrational and scientifically unsupportable. Pediatrics, of course, will disappear as more and more mothers are encouraged to breastfeed their babies.

The New Doctor is committed not only to putting the specialists out of business, but to putting himself out of business as well. Doctors used to say they were in business to put themselves out of business, but it was only a slogan. Now you don't even hear them saying it anymore. But the New Doctor will back up his commitment with action. He or she will teach people how to keep themselves healthy and how to restore health and balance without the aid of a professional. While the New Doctor knows there will always be a need for doctors, the doctor's role in the person's health will diminish to the point where it might not be a bad idea if doctors had another way to earn a living besides practicing medicine. One thing is certain, if every doctor were a New Doctor, we would need far fewer doctors and medical care would not be the outsized behemoth in people's lives that it is today.

The New Doctor must be prepared for courageous behavior, which means doing what has to be done even though it means giving up the wealth, power, and status associated with being a conventional physician. I don't think we'll have any trouble instilling courage in New Doctors. The ones I've met—as both doctors and doctors-to-be—seem to come equipped with both courage and the cunning to defend themselves. I met a young doctor recently who had quit his formal medical education as soon as he was eligible for a license—immediately after his internship. I asked him where he was licensed, and he told me in *five* states. He said he anticipated having trouble with the medical establishment, so he's prepared if they start taking his license away. Smartest fellow I've met in a long time. The New Doctor knows what he has to do to survive long enough to work himself out of business.

Obviously, the New Doctor exists *despite* his or her medical education rather than because of it. With this in mind, I and a number of my colleagues have created a blueprint for the New Medical School, which is now actively seeking state approval and looking forward to taking on its first class of New Doctors-to-be.

The education of the New Doctor will include not only medical and clinical sciences but ethics and literature as well. All students in the New Medical School will be shown how human behavior relates to health and disease. New Doctors will be trained to communicate by means of the written as well as the spoken word. They also will learn the basic techniques and social implications of other media, such as television. New Doctors must not only be able to communicate effectively with the community, but they must be aware of the processes by which they and their patients are influenced. Since legal procedures are important not only to the doctor's protection of his practice but to the protection of his patients as well, New Doctors will learn to deal with lawyers and the law.

The New Medical School will have a Department of Ethics and Justice. A community's concept of justice determines the health of its members in terms of life expectancy, infant mortality, morbidity statistics, and quality of medical care. Theoretical economic structures are irrelevant. A free enterprise system saturated with justice can provide good medical care, while a socialized medical system devoid of justice can provide deadly medical care. An immoral society that sets arbitrary limits on technological achievements can be harmful, while a moral society that strives for the best that technology has to offer can produce healthy people. In our Department of Ethics, the traditional medical disciplines will be required to expose their material to the light of various ethical systems: Jewish, Christian, Hindu, Islamic, utilitarian, situational, etc.

The New Medical School will have a very strong Department of Iatrogenic Disease. In this department all medical disciplines and specialties will be required to demonstrate how their methods can produce disease and disability. Doctors and professors will be paid to find out how medical care does more harm than good, and how proposed new treatments might prove harmful.

Instead of the New Medical School providing the same specialist-encouraging instruction and role models that conventional schools do, it will stress generalism. The New Medical School will be an open forum of ideas on healing. Students will be taught not only by medical doctors, but by osteopaths and chiropractors and naturopaths and nutritionists. We don't want the New Doctors to learn about these ideas and practices as if they were abstract academic principles. We want them to see them practiced firsthand.

The New Doctor will be educated in methods and principles that do not become obsolete every few years. Once the fifty-to-ninety percent of what is now being taught is rejected as either wrong, outdated or irrelevant, we will have enough time to teach what has to be taught, such as fundamentals of diagnosis and prognosis.

The New Medical School will begin producing New Doctors by selecting a different kind of person to be a student. Students who score highly on traditional medical school entrance exams tend to be too compulsively achievement-oriented. They lose contact with the genuine goals of medicine and become wrapped up in competition and in the application of technology to *subdue* rather than restore the balance of Nature. The New Medical School will downplay quantitative tests and look for people who are comfortable being with people rather than doing something for or to them. We don't want insecure people with so little self-esteem that they always need to be proving themselves by challenging their peers and defending their status. Such characters are unhealthy to those around them as well as to themselves.

To help avoid the social pathology that seems to affect physicians as a group, the New Medical School will concern itself with supporting and strengthening the family life of each New Doctor. We will encourage students to marry and have families, because we want them to experience their profession from both sides, as real people. The New Doctor will also have strong roots in the community, since the local culture of a people is always a factor in health and disease.

I remember some years back I was asked to give the speech to incoming medical students at a medical school. The title of my talk was "How To Survive Medical School." I gave them a number of rules, one of which was to stay close to your family and to people you knew before medical school. Stay close to people who are not doctors and not studying to be doctors. Don't work too hard. Don't try for A's. It's almost impossible to get kicked out of medical school, so you might as well just slide through. Make a major investment in your education, but not an exclusive one. Not an investment to the exclusion of the rest of your life.

After I finished, the dean of the school got up and said he agreed with everything I said, but that the students should always remember that when you enter medicine you are entering a *new life!*

Students at the New Medical School will be taught in a different manner, too. Their relationship to the faculty will be as graduate students actively involved in the study of a discipline rather than as passive recipients of trade school training. The New Medical School will not be a research institution or a hospital. It will be a *school*. Students will be assigned to teachers, not to hospitals. The teaching format will be by preceptorship or professional apprenticeship. Students will take responsibility for their own education.

When those young men and women are graduated, you won't have any trouble distinguishing them from the rest of the pack. For in preparing the state application form for our New Medical School, we visited a number of other medical schools. One of them was a new school in a small community in southern Illinois. After they had finished showing us all they had accomplished, we asked the directors one question: If you were to mix your graduates with a bunch of Harvard Medical School graduates, would you be able to tell them apart? The answer was "No, you wouldn't, because our students are indistinguishable from those at Harvard."

We then decided that we wanted nothing further to do with that school. Our students are going to be easily identifiable:

Their first rule is going to be *First, Do No Harm.*

Bibliography

I have purposely omitted references from the text itself or in foot-notes for three reasons:

1. To avoid interfering with the reader's concentration on the book itself.

2. In the belief that the major ideas in the book can stand on common sense, independently of the reference sources.

3. Documentation of the failure of American medicine is, in 1979, widely publicized and well known.

Nevertheless, for those who are interested in those sources which support my book, I recommend about 100 hours of reading:

1. There are dozens of anti-doctor books easily available. My favorites, from the standpoint of comprehensive documentation and literary elegance are:

The Medicine Men by Leonard Tushnet, M.D., St. Martin's Press, 1971. (Available through Caveat Emptor, 620 Freeman Street, Orange, N.J. 07050.)

Medical Nemesis by Ivan Illich, Pantheon Press, 1976.

Modern Medical Mistakes by Edward C. Lambert, M.D., Indiana University Press, 1978.

2. One of the best critiques of modern preventive medicine is:

Presymptomatic Detection and Early Diagnosis by C.L. Sharp and Harry Keen, Williams and Wilkins, 1968.

3. My favorite critiques of psychiatry and psychoanalysis are:

Coping with Psychiatric and Psychological Testimony by Jay Ziskin, LL.B., Ph.D. (clinical psychology), Law and Psychology Press, Beverly Hills, 1975.

The Psychological Society by Martin Gross, Random House, 1978.

4. Of the many references on ethics and its relation to medicine, I have selected from my own religious tradition:

Jewish Medical Ethics by Immanuel Jakobovits, Bloch Publishing, New York, 1975.

Modern Medicine and Jewish Law by Fred Rosner, M.D., Bloch Publishing, New York, 1972.

Marital Relations, Birth Control and Abortion in Jewish Law by David Feldman, Schocken Books, 1974.

5. Finally, my monthly subscription newsletter, "The Peoples Doctor" (Vera Chatz, Associate Editor, 664 N. Michigan Avenue, Chicago IL 60611) provides an on-going source of authoritative documentation.

Organizations

Prenatal Care

Society for the Protection of the Unborn through Nutrition (SPUN); Tom Brewer, M.D., President, author (with Gail Brewer) of *What Every Pregnant Woman Should Know* (Random House, New York, 1977).

Childbirth

National Association of Parents and Professionals for Safe Alternatives in Childbirth (NAPSAC); President, David Stewart, editor of *Safe Alternatives in Childbirth* (NAPSAC, Chapel Hill, North Carolina, 1976) and *Twenty-first Century Obstetrics Now!* (NAPSAC, Chapel Hill, North Carolina, 1977).

Infant Feeding and Mothering

La Leche League; President, Marian Tompson; major publication "The Womanly Art of Breastfeeding" (LLL, Franklin Park, Illinois, 1958, revised 1963).

Index